© Cherie Fournier

ABOUT THE AUTHOR

Corrine Kenner specializes in bringing metaphysical subjects down to earth. She's a world-renowned expert on tarot and astrology, with a degree in philosophy from California State University. She's written more than two dozen guidebooks on tarot and astrology, and she's created several best-selling tarot decks. Most of her work has been translated for a global audience; her publications are available in sixteen languages.

gently HAUNTED

TRUE STORIES FROM THE HAUNTED ANTIQUE SHOP

Llewellyn Publications
Woodbury, Minnesotas

FIRST EDITION
First Printing, 2022

Cover design by Cassie Willett
Interior photo credits on page 205

Llewellyn Publications is a registered trademark of Llewellyn Worldwide Ltd.

Library of Congress Cataloging-in-Publication Data (Pending)
ISBN: 978-0-7387-7181-6

Llewellyn Worldwide Ltd. does not participate in, endorse, or have any authority or responsibility concerning private business transactions between our authors and the public.

All mail addressed to the author is forwarded but the publisher cannot, unless specifically instructed by the author, give out an address or phone number.

Any internet references contained in this work are current at publication time, but the publisher cannot guarantee that a specific location will continue to be maintained. Please refer to the publisher's website for links to authors' websites and other sources.

Llewellyn Publications
A Division of Llewellyn Worldwide Ltd.
2143 Wooddale Drive
Woodbury, MN 55125-2989
www.llewellyn.com

Printed in the United States of America

OTHER WORKS BY CORRINE KENNER

Afterthoughts: A Guide to the After Tarot

Astrology for Writers: Spark Your Creativity Using the Zodiac

The Colors of Light: A Guide to the Impressionist Tarot

Crystals for Beginners: A Guide to Collecting & Using Stones & Crystals

Epicurean Tarot Recipe Cards

Flash Fiction: Mix-and-Match Writing Prompts

Foresight: A Guide to the Before Tarot

Simple Fortunetelling with Tarot Cards: Corrine Kenner's Complete Guide

The Ghosts of Devils Lake: True Stories from My Haunted Hometown

Strange But True: True Stories from the Files of FATE Magazine (co-editor)

Susan and the Mermaid (edited with commentary)

Tall Dark Stranger: Tarot for Love and Romance

Tarot and Astrology: Enhance Your Readings with the Wisdom of the Zodiac

Tarot for Writers

Tarot Journaling: Using the Celtic Cross to Unveil Your Hidden Story

The Wandering Stars Tarot

Wizards Tarot

FICTION WORKS (WRITING AS CIELLE KENNER)

The Ghost of Griffith Park

Stolen Moments: Flash Fiction Stories and Poems

DEDICATION

To everyone who visits the
Haunted Antique Shop,
in body and in spirit.

CONTENTS

INTRODUCTION

WELCOME TO THE HAUNTED ANTIQUE SHOP!

Have you ever found yourself in an antique store, drawn to an old photo that stopped you in your tracks because it looked so familiar? Have you ever felt like a vintage book, timeworn furniture, or heirloom jewelry was calling out to you?

You're not alone. Antiques aren't just remnants of the past. They're artifacts, imbued with the energy and emotions of people who treasured them and preserved them for future generations—and they represent a direct connection to the past.

Some antiques are intrinsically valuable because they were crafted from gold or silver. Some have sentimental appeal because they're mementos of other times and other places. Either way, they're tangible reminders of the fact that the past is always present—and as one day leads to the next, our memories of the past can ease our transition into the future too.

My name is Corrine Kenner. I'm an author, astrologer, certified tarot master, and owner of the Haunted Antique Shop, which, true to its name, is a gently haunted antique shop in DeLand, Florida. It's a place where the past, present, and future coexist, and even skeptics find themselves connecting with the Spirit World.

Image 1: The Haunted Antique Shop is based in a historic craftsman bungalow in DeLand, Florida.

In the following pages, I'll tell you about some of the supernatural events I've experienced here, along with the haunted history of our small town in Central Florida. I'll also show you how you can reach out to the Other Side yourself, wherever you happen to be. I'll offer you tools and techniques for spirit contact along with tips and hints I've learned along the way.

But first, let me tell you a little about how the Haunted Antique Shop came to be.

CHAPTER 1
THE HAUNTED ANTIQUE SHOP

COME IN! WE'RE GENTLY HAUNTED.

I never planned to be the proprietor of a haunted antique shop—or any retail business, for that matter. I'm a writer, and when I first came across the shop for sale, I was actually looking for office space.

My husband, Dan, and I moved to DeLand in 2017. We're both from Minnesota, but after too many long, cold winters, we came to Florida for the promise of perpetual summer. While we settled into our new life, I worked from our living room—but after a few months, I wanted a space where I could write full time, professionally.

I didn't want to open a new business, learn a new trade, or make a major investment in a new field. I just wanted a little place where I could put words on paper. Like Virginia Woolf, all I wanted was a room of my own.

But as I searched for office space to rent, I came across a listing for a cozy-looking shop called the Vintage Cottage two blocks from my house. The owner, a woman named Carmen, had built it up over the course of a year, filling it with vintage clothing, jewelry, artwork, and accessories. She had a flair for design and display, so all of her merchandise was artfully arranged on antique fixtures and furnishings, including old-fashioned mannequins and dress forms. In addition to an office space, there was room for meetings too, so I could host a writers group, a book club, writing classes, and workshops. I was inspired from the moment I walked through the door.

Image 2: At the Haunted Antique Shop, we're surrounded by spirits of the past.

What's more, the location was ideal. Not only was it close to home, but the shop was situated on one of the city's main thoroughfares, where thousands of cars pass by each day. The price was right too. Most turnkey businesses cost as much as a house—well into the six figures. This one, lock, stock, and barrel, was eight thousand dollars, which was more like the cost of a used car. The building was leased, but that lease was transferable, and the property owner seemed amenable.

So what was the catch? Just one, really: the shop was bleeding money. Customers would straggle in, but most of them were bargain hunters making the rounds of thrift stores in the area. They would spend a dollar here or there, but a twenty-dollar sale was a monumental achievement. There were many days when no one even walked through the door. There was no way that sales revenue could even come close to covering the cost of the lease or utilities.

The shop wasn't a sound business investment—but then again, I wasn't looking for a business investment. I was looking for a place to write.

It didn't take much time to do the math. Rent for the entire property was just a little more than a single room in an office building. I was pretty sure I could recoup some of that cost by selling antiques. I knew I could write when the shop was empty and take breaks from my writing whenever customers happened to wander in. And given that my expenses would be about the same either way, I decided to see where the shop would take me.

I never could have guessed that it would take me into another world.

ON-THE-JOB TRAINING

At first, I pictured myself carrying on as a simple, small-town shopkeeper, focused on antiques. Of course, I knew there would be a learning curve. It might even be somewhat steep.

After all, did I have a business plan? No. Did I know how to run a business? No. Did I know accounting or bookkeeping? No. Did I have ongoing funds for marketing, maintenance, and merchandise? Also no. Did I know anything about antiques? Not really, but I knew I could learn on the job, researching merchandise as I went along. Thanks to the internet, that part is actually pretty easy.

I had also inherited great wisdom from my great-aunt Dorothy, who had dabbled in the antique business. Aside from marrying rich men who died young, she had long ago told me her secret to success. "Corrine," she'd say, "all you really need is orange oil. Whenever you find antique furniture, just polish it with orange oil."

TAROT AND ASTROLOGY

While it sounds crazy now, I didn't plan to offer psychic readings at the shop. I'd written several books on astrology and tarot, but I thought I was moving away from that part of my life. I wanted to delve into new genres, learn new skills, and broaden my repertoire. I wanted to be a creative writer, exploring new realms of insight and imagination. I wanted to be a novelist!

I still do—but once I bought the shop, I discovered that the Spirit World had additional plans for me.

When I first started my writing career, I worked as a newspaper reporter. Later, I moved into magazine editing, book publishing, and web design. And somewhere along the way, I also discovered tarot and astrology.

The images and symbols weren't completely foreign to me. Back when I was earning a degree in philosophy, the myths and legends of the ancient Greeks were a major part of the curriculum.

Over the years, I came to rely on tarot and astrology for creative inspiration. I think tarot cards are a visual tool that helps us see our own life in pictures, while the symbolism of astrology helps us understand our place in the grand scheme of the universe.

As I set up shop, friends and relatives nudged me a bit, wondering out loud if I would sell my tarot and astrology books there too. I knew that was a possibility, but I hesitated. I was fairly new to town, and I hadn't met many people yet. Putting my publications on display would put me out there as some sort of New-Age mystic, and I wasn't sure I wanted to do that. I wanted to focus on fiction, and I wanted to finish a novel I had started. If that was my plan, no one needed to know what I had written before.

I also had to consider the fact that DeLand is somewhat conservative—more like Memphis than Miami. I didn't want to wave red flags at my new neighbors, many of whom are fundamentalists. What if some random churchgoer accused me of witchcraft? What if some of them decided to picket my shop? That would be awkward.

Even so, it was my shop, and in theory, I could do what I wanted with it.

That's when I realized that antique shops are always haunted. If they're not inhabited by actual ghosts, they're at least inhabited by the spirits of the past. The more I thought about it, the more I realized that I could embrace the idea and make it central to my marketing.

HAUNTED ANTIQUES

When I first bought the shop, Carmen was excited about my marketing plans. I had told her about some of my work with tarot and astrology, as well as my books.

Image 3: This portrait of a newlywed couple has been hanging in the Haunted Antique Shop since it opened.

As soon as I signed the paperwork that transferred ownership, she pulled a vintage wedding portrait off the wall and asked me to read it psychically.

"Who are these people?" she asked. "Can you get their names? Where were they from?" She didn't know anything about the photo, and she was curious.

Suddenly, I was on the spot. I was already feeling overwhelmed by the whole transaction. I had just bought a business I probably had no business buying, and while it wasn't my *entire* life savings, I had just plunked down a good chunk of change. What's more, I had committed to keeping the shop going for at least a year, when the lease would be up for renewal.

Well … in for a penny, in for a pound.

Right there, in my first few minutes as the owner of a haunted antique shop, I started to devise my own method of assessing the psychic stories behind our merchandise.

I held the photo in my hands, resting the bottom of the frame in my lap. I closed my eyes and tried to clear my mind. Those are the first steps in the process of psychometry—the art of gleaning psychic information through touch. I sat still, and suddenly, two names popped into my head: Frank and Genovesa. I wasn't even sure if Genovesa was a name, but the more I focused on it, the more it seemed to fit. As I continued to sit, holding the portrait, waiting for information, I heard orchestral music playing faintly. Was that their wedding song?

Psychometry isn't my strongest suit, so I augmented the reading with tarot cards. I shuffled and two cards fell out of the deck: the Hermit for the groom and the Star for the bride.

The Hermit depicts a cloaked man standing on a mountaintop, holding a lantern that glows with the light of a single star. The Star card shows a woman kneeling by a pond, illuminated by a sky filled with stars. Stars are symbols of hope and inspiration, reflecting the light of a distant sun and traveling from the past to illuminate our present.

That seemed to fit too. If nothing else, the cards described the couple's shared affection for one another and suggested that the groom continued to carry a torch for his bride.

As time has passed, I still rely on psychometry and tarot for insight into the antiques I sell, but I've added other tools to our psychic tool kit. Those include Spirit Key pendulums, dowsing rods, and astrology charts, if I happen to know times, dates, and locations associated with the merchandise. I can't always verify the information, but it usually aligns closely with the historical research I do when I assess each piece.

MARKETING FOR MYSTICS

When I first bought the shop, I kept the Vintage Cottage name, but I added a new slogan: the Haunted Antique Shop.

I also decided to put just a few of my books on a corner shelf. I didn't face them out to the world, with the covers on full display, because that would be too brazen. I simply tucked them next to some silver candlesticks, looking for all the world like props, not products.

When customers stopped to ask me about the collection, I'd shrug and laugh a little and say, "Oh, those are just some books I wrote."

Then they'd study the covers, which are self-explanatory: *Tarot for Writers. Astrology for Writers. Tarot and Astrology.* The titles aren't clever, but they're clear.

Much to my relief, nobody recoiled. What's more, nobody knocked the books to the floor in disgust, and nobody demanded that they be burned in a pile on the street. Instead, people got excited. "You wrote these books?" they said. *"You're* the author?" Then they started picking them up, flipping through the pages, and asking if I could sign them. Some people even asked for readings.

I had done professional readings in the past. Back when I was writing most of my tarot and astrology books, I offered consultations from a metaphysical shop in Minneapolis. Working there, on call to walk-in clients, was a great way to test my theories and practices surrounding the cards.

I remembered how good it felt to be of service to people with serious questions, so I decided to create a reading space at the Haunted Antique Shop too. I didn't want it to be too flashy, though. I still wasn't ready to go all in.

My first attempt failed miserably. In hindsight, I suppose it was predictable, because I was still trying to keep it low-key. I set up a little table in my office because the rest of the shop was full. Unfortunately, my desk is usually covered in paperwork and untagged merchandise, so it wasn't particularly inviting, and I was usually too self-conscious to invite people in. I did a few readings in my office on days when I felt confident that the room was clean enough for company, but I knew something had to change.

I carried on for a few months, periodically doing readings in my office, the dining room, or the front parlor, depending on time and traffic through the shop.

Then Covid hit.

Like many businesses around the country, I closed up shop—at first for two weeks, and then two more weeks, and then another month. As the days passed, while everyone waited for the all clear when the world would return to normal, I pondered ways to keep the business alive.

At some point during the pandemic, I realized that I could lean into the mystique of the Haunted Antique Shop—not just as a slogan but as a brand. After all, the virus had effectively shut down the economy anyway. I had nothing to lose.

It was oddly liberating. I filed official paperwork to change my business name. I designed new signs, revamped the website, and amped up our social media. I put all my books on full display, and I cleared one room of the shop completely to make space for a dedicated tarot parlor. I also decided to put more emphasis on the haunted antiques in our collection so visitors could glean even more insight into the Spirit World.

THE TAROT PARLOR

And what happened?

Florida reopened, and business boomed. In a time of turmoil, I found customers eager for a reminder that life goes on and that our connections with the infinite are eternal.

These days, it's not unusual to have new customers walk through the door, breathless with excitement. "As soon as I saw your sign," they say, "I did a U-turn right in the middle of the street. I love this stuff!"

I'm not going to tell you that I've become the world's best businessperson in the process. Nothing could be further from the truth; the learning curve *is* steep, and I'm still working on basic skills that other entrepreneurs probably take for granted. Sometimes I forget what I'm doing at the cash register, and I have to clear a pending transaction and start over. I'm terrible at counting change; after all, I'm a writer, not a mathematician. I even struggle a bit when I need to wrap or package merchandise, especially if it's very old or fragile.

Image 4: Our tarot parlor is a magical place for psychic readings.

I've also tried quite a few marketing ideas that have flopped spectacularly, like ad campaigns that led nowhere and events that generated absolutely no interest. More than once, I've set up our meeting space for a workshop or discussion group, only to find myself sitting alone, eating the cookies I'd set out for a crowd. I don't count those experiences as failures, though. They're experiments, and each one leads to discoveries of what works—and what doesn't.

But all in all, the shop has become a destination for kindred spirits, and we stay pretty busy. My husband and daughters come in to help sometimes, which also makes it feel more like a family project than a business endeavor. We like meeting new people, welcoming them into the shop, and sharing all the unusual things we have to offer.

OUR HAUNTED HEADQUARTERS

Be it ever so haunted, there's no place like home.

Step into the Haunted Antique Shop, and you'll feel like you've stepped back in time. You'll be surrounded by antiques and memorabilia that were loved and cherished by earlier generations in a historic home that still looks like it did a hundred years ago.

Image 5: Back when the Haunted Antique Shop was a family home, it had a grassy front lawn and a screened-in porch. This photo was taken sometime before 1992.

You'll also find yourself surrounded by spirits.

Some are the ghosts of those who treasured the objects in our collection. Some are returning to the house itself because they lived and worked here. And some come through the door with living visitors, joining them in spirit, hoping to reconnect.

None of the spirits are malevolent—but many are mischievous. It's not uncommon to find merchandise mysteriously rearranged during the dark of night. Doors open and close on their own. Lights turn on and off, seemingly of their own accord. When I'm in the office or the back room, the front door often chimes as if customers have come in—but when I go to greet them, no one is there. And on quiet weekend afternoons, when the traffic outside comes to a lull, I hear the sound of horses and wagons on the street, just as we would have heard a century ago.

We think we have at least five resident spirits at the shop, all of whom used to live here when they were alive. James and Lucinda DeWalt were the first couple to move in. They were followed by many others, including James and Rossie Hearne, who had mother-in-law problems, and Annette Dennis, who was—and is—musically inclined. You'll meet them all in the next section.

Image 6: The Haunted Antique Shop is part of the West DeLand Residential District, which was added to the National Register of Historic Places in 1992.

The house itself is a craftsman bungalow that was built in 1921. It's a tidy little structure. The high ceilings, plaster walls, and gleaming hardwood floors muffle the sounds of the outside world, while lace curtains filter the Florida sun. Customers visibly relax when they walk through the door. Many say it's like walking into a favorite grandmother's house.

That's not a coincidence. The shop's decor is modeled after my great-grandmother's house in Minneapolis, which was built during the same time frame. The basic architectural elements are similar, from the pine floors to the plaster walls and coved ceilings.

The rooms are still laid out like a family home, even though no one lives there anymore. (No one in corporeal form, at least.) When you visit, you'll walk up the steps, across the front porch, and through the front door. You'll find yourself in the front parlor—a warm and welcoming space, with a mahogany table that's often set for tea, and a fireplace in the corner. Thanks to the modern miracle of electric logs, we keep the fireplace lit. Pause for a moment, and you'll see and hear the crackling of flames in the hearth.

Look to your left, and you'll see two smaller rooms that used to be bedrooms. Today we use the first bedroom as the tarot parlor and the second bedroom as an office.

Walk on through, and you'll find yourself in the dining room. It's still furnished with a traditional table and chairs, and we gather there for classes, workshops, and special events.

The original kitchen is in the back. We use that room to display vintage dinnerware and primitive kitchen tools. They're all hallmarks of a time when ordinary objects were works of art.

The Haunted Antique Shop seems to get more haunted with every passing day. I think that's because we're creating a space where unusual activity and events are not only allowed, but welcome and invited. That psychic energy we create doesn't just invite the ghosts we already know. It also serves as a beacon to other curious, good-natured spirits.

I am pretty careful about the merchandise I bring into the shop. I like oddities, but not gruesome discoveries. I like hauntings, but not horror. And while I know that a lot of people love a good scare, that's a line I don't want to cross. That's because I truly believe that surrounding yourself with violent imagery and macabre memorabilia will elevate your stress and send your psyche into shock. A good scare, like a good cry, can be cathartic. A good fright can reaffirm your love of life—but it's not healthy to mainline horror. Like a drug, you'll need more and more to keep the high.

For that reason, all of the antiques we have on hand are pieces that feel good. We never deal in objects that are shrouded in negativity. We've been offered relics with a dark energy and objects that seem to have frightening specters attached to them. We've even been offered a genuine human skull.

We pass every time. We're not interested in taking possession of entities we wouldn't invite into our lives or our homes.

CHAPTER 2

RESIDENT SPIRITS

DeLand is a magical place, nestled along the St. Johns River and surrounded by old-growth national forests. The city's founders were adventurers who settled here after the Civil War. Instead of heading west like so many other pioneers at the time, they moved south, staking claims in Central Florida—which, until then, was thought to be uninhabitable.

Those early homesteaders had more than a dream: they had a vision. Starting with their first town meeting in a log cabin, they created a master plan for their community. Their goal was to design a city that would serve as a center for art and culture. From the start, they billed it as "The Athens of Florida."

Today, their vision is alive and well. DeLand might be a small town, but it's home to a university and a technical college, several museums, and a historic theater. Its award-winning main street is lined with picturesque shops and family-owned restaurants. On weekends, you'll find farmer's markets, craft shows, art festivals, and live music that make the town a popular destination for day trips. And even though the town is bustling, the pace is comfortable and relaxed. While the Haunted Antique Shop will take you back a hundred years, you'll feel time start to slow down as soon as you drive into town.

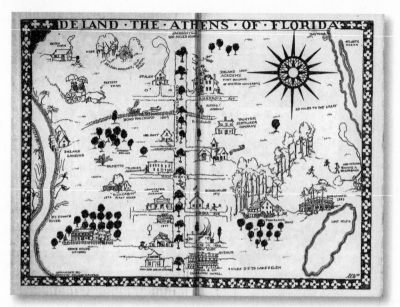

Image 7: An early history of DeLand, published in 1928, included a hand-drawn map of the town.

DeLand is located thirty-five miles north of Orlando, twenty miles west of Daytona Beach, and five miles from Cassadaga, a historic Spiritualist community.

HOME AT LAST

Back in 1920, when the Haunted Antique Shop was newly built, a couple named James and Lucinda DeWalt were the first to call it home. They probably moved in before the paint was even dry on the plaster walls.

Their bungalow was one of thousands built during a Florida land boom that followed World War I. At the time, houses were going up as fast as builders could hammer them together. As I write this, the same thing is happening now.

James and Lucinda were living in an era of unbounded prosperity. The roaring twenties were just getting into full swing, which meant the whole country was enjoying a cultural renaissance of music, dance, and entertainment that promised to lighten the burdens of everyday life.

Back then, the future held nothing but promise. From their covered front porch, James and Lucinda had a sweeping view of DeLand's tree-lined lanes. Towering oaks arched over streets and sidewalks, creating a living canopy of shade and shelter. The long, leafy branches were made even more beautiful by strands of silvery Spanish moss that shimmered in the sunlight and swayed in the breeze.

James and Lucinda thought their future was assured. They probably planned to live the rest of their days in their new home, enjoying their time together, and marveling at all the new technology that would make life better. Automobiles had revolutionized transportation. Silent movies were bringing the best and brightest stars to every small town in America, including DeLand. Radio broadcasts promised to bring the world's greatest musicians and storytellers into their own front parlor. They probably could have imagined themselves sitting on their front porch for decades to come.

Image 8: James and Lucinda DeWalt were the first to live in the Haunted Antique Shop, when it was a newly built home on this tree-lined Florida street. It seems they never left.

James, a chauffeur, probably drove a Ford. He would have worked most nights, driving winter tourists to performances at the nearby Athens Theatre or dinner at the College Arms Hotel. He also would have worn the standard chauffeur's uniform of the time: a cap, black coat, knee breeches, tall boots, and gauntlet gloves. At the time, chauffeurs wore legally mandated badges too, which were like driver's licenses that verified their training and status.

While her husband worked, Lucinda would have waited for him at home in a rocking chair by the fireplace. She would have whiled away the hours doing needlework, writing letters, or reading. DeLand always had several newspapers and a well-stocked library, and magazines were sold at shops all across town.

We still have a rocking chair in the front room, exactly where Lucinda would have had her chair. Our rocker sometimes moves gently on its own, as if she's still there, still waiting for her husband to come home. We see it shifting ever so slightly, and the effect is oddly soothing. When it rocks, I always make it a point to say hello, just as I say goodbye to her when I leave the shop at night.

"Lucinda's chair," as I call it, is vintage, but it's not particularly old. Based on its markings, I think it's a reproduction that was manufactured in the 1970s, when Americans celebrated the bicentennial history of our country and historic furnishings were in fashion. Even so, the rocker looks and feels like a genuine antique, crafted from heavy maple, painted with black lacquer, and stenciled with gold leaf.

It's easy to picture Lucinda there, listening for the sound of James's car in the gravel driveway, signaling his return. After he parked behind the house, she would have heard his footsteps on the back porch. He'd call out quietly as he opened the back door, not wanting to startle her, but not wanting to wake her, either, if she happened to be asleep.

These days, we think it's James's voice we hear in the back room, in what used to be the pantry. I've heard it. So have my daughters. Some of our customers have heard it as well—especially if they happen to be using the ghost hunting kit we keep near the front door.

Visitors who try our dowsing rods are invariably led through the parlor, the dining room, the original kitchen, all the way back to the old pantry at the rear of the shop. It's not much to look at. The room is small and windowless, with a sloped ceiling. We use it as a kitchenette, with a refrigerator and microwave to heat our lunches.

Most visitors who find themselves there are a little confused at first. They can't understand why they're being shown a basic, utilitarian space when they're in a shop full of haunted antiques.

Everyone who hears him reports the same thing: James's voice is calm, quiet, and deep, like a baritone. Sometimes he clears his throat, as if he's gently letting us know we're not alone. Sometimes he simply says, "Hey," like a greeting. Each time, his voice is as clear and audible as a living man's.

In my mind's eye, I can picture James clearly. He's not particularly tall. He's maybe 5 feet, 8 inches, but he stands straight, and his shoulders are broad. He wears wire-rim glasses with round lenses, but he assures me he didn't need them to drive. He believes men should never leave home without a hat, and he doesn't understand why so many men today don't recognize the aesthetic appeal of a good fedora. His presence is every bit as warm and welcoming as his wife's.

Is he talking to us, or is he back at the shop to be with Lucinda? I think it's both. James knows his wife is nearby, but he's still in service mode. When customers call, as they did in his chauffeur days, he stands willing and ready to escort them to their destination. By offering a kind word or two in the Haunted Antique Shop, he's showing us the way to the Other Side.

While they still haunt the shop, no one really knows what happened to James and Lucinda. Maybe James got sick. Maybe they lost their life savings at the end of the 1920s, when the stock market crashed, the banks collapsed, and the world was plunged into a deep and lasting Great Depression. Whatever the case, James and Lucinda didn't let misfortune force them from their home. They chose to stay long after their corporeal forms were dead and gone.

And now, just as in life, James and Lucinda continue to enjoy the porch, watching clouds drift lazily by until the sun sets in a riot of Florida reds, oranges, purples, and blues. Some nights, after we close the shop, we join them. We sit back with iced tea or a glass of wine and count our blessings.

We almost never feel as though we're sitting there alone. We know we share the space with any number of ghosts from the past, all with their own memories, dreams, and reflections.

THE CABINET OF CURIOSITIES

We keep our most haunted artifacts in our Cabinet of Curiosities. Its shelves are filled with an ever-changing array of intriguing collectibles, including dolls, ceramic figurines, vintage toys, and old photos.

Image 9: The Cabinet of Curiosities is filled with our most haunted artifacts.

The cabinet itself is an antique wardrobe with mirrored doors that creak when they're opened. The side panels are attached with iron pins, an age-old method of building furniture so it can be disassembled, broken down, and carried up staircases and through narrow passageways.

Some people say the Cabinet of Curiosities looks like the oversized wardrobe from *Beauty and the Beast*. Others are reminded of the magical portal to Narnia in *The Lion, the Witch, and the Wardrobe*. Either way, its mysterious allure is unmistakable.

Almost everyone hesitates before they open the Cabinet of Curiosities. It could be that they sense the aura of magic that emanates from inside. It might also be the warning sign we've hung from one of the doors. "Caution," it reads, "extremely haunted. Open if you dare."

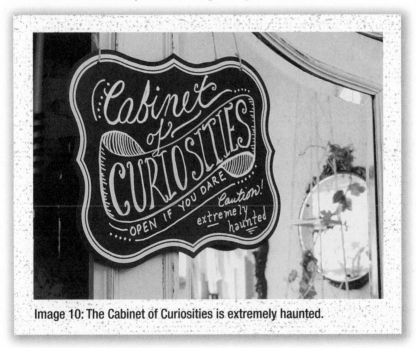

Image 10: The Cabinet of Curiosities is extremely haunted.

That caveat might not be necessary, especially in the Haunted Antique Shop, where everything in the store could have a ghost attached. Even so, it's fair warning. I usually need to take a deep breath myself, because there's no telling what we'll find once the doors are opened.

Some of the objects inside move on their own, so we might need to reposition them before customers come in. Others seem to radiate mischief. One doll has eyes that follow visitors around the room. Another smiles when she sees newcomers. Old playing cards and poker chips are embedded with a gambler's spirit still hoping to strike it rich, while a collection of antique medicine bottles reminds us of the ailments and misfortunes of a bygone time.

People do say they feel psychic energy radiating from the cabinet, as if more than one spirit is occupying the space. A few people have even had to step outside, sit in the chairs on our front porch, and take a few deep breaths before they come back into the shop. They don't want to leave; they just need a moment to center themselves before they dive back into the experience. We keep bottled water and cookies on hand for extra-sensitive guests who need help getting grounded.

When we get new merchandise, we research it, just as any antique dealer would. We ask questions and try to get as much information as possible from the sellers or donors. We study labels and maker's marks and research them online. We set our asking prices based on comparable products on auction and antique sites.

Then we take it a step further. Because we have a staff of psychics on hand, we can turn to pendulums, dowsing rods, tarot cards, and psychometry to tune in to the energy of the objects on our shelves.

When one of our acquisitions feels particularly haunted, we give it a place of honor in the cabinet. We also use EMF meters to choose objects for the display.

EMF meters are sophisticated instruments that measure electromagnetic fields around electrical devices and equipment, including electric wiring, power lines, and transformers. Normally, seemingly inert objects like stuffed animals or glass bottles wouldn't emit any measurable electromagnetism—but at the Haunted Antique Shop, they do.

Everything in the cabinet has set off the EMF meter at least once, but they don't all emit psychic energy all the time. I think that's because spirits are free to come and go at will. In any case, our customers like to use EMF meters to scan the shelves for themselves, to see which items are most active at any given moment. Once they're done with the cabinet, they fan out and survey the other rooms in the shop too.

Most of the items in the Cabinet of Curiosities seem content behind the closed doors. Only a few make it clear that they'd rather be left out in the open—like Haunted Charlie, the doll you'll meet in the next story.

To date, we've only had one truly unsettling experience with the Cabinet of Curiosities. Two women came into the shop while I happened to be in Orlando, forty minutes away. My daughter Emily was minding the store. I was about to head home when she called in a panic.

"Mom," she pleaded. "You've got to come take care of this Cabinet of Curiosities. We had some ladies in the shop, and when they opened it, it smelled terrible. I mean, it's really bad. I don't know what it was. I think maybe you've got a dead mouse in there. It was awful. I could smell it across the room."

I was mortified. I want all of our customers to have a good experience, and dead mice don't fall into the category of charming shopping adventures.

"Did you look inside?"

"No way. I don't want to see what it is."

"Do you smell it now?"

"No, but I opened the front door and sprayed air freshener and lit candles, and I think that helped."

"What happened to the ladies?"

"Well, they kind of jumped back at the smell and slammed the doors shut. It still smelled really bad, though...like death. They looked around for a minute, but then they said they couldn't take it and they left."

I rushed back to DeLand and headed straight to the shop. When I walked in, I couldn't smell anything but lavender oil from the diffusers we always use.

Warily, I opened the cabinet and peeked inside. Everything looked fine, and I still couldn't smell anything bad.

I moved a few things around to see if there could have been a dead mouse or a salamander or some other odd little Florida creature tucked away behind one of the antiques. I used a flashlight to peer into the corners. There was nothing. The cabinet is essentially a wood box with shelves, so there are no compartments or cubbyholes where anything could hide.

"Emily," I asked, "did those women say anything else while they were here?"

"Not really," she said. "Only that one of them is haunted, and she has a ghost attached to her."

Well, that was a part of the story I wished I had known before I went screaming down the I-4 corridor.

"She said her attic smells like that too."

I breathed a deep sigh of relief. Not for the woman, because whoever or whatever she was dealing with didn't sound fun. But as far as the shop was concerned, I figured we were in the clear.

"Well," I said, "if she had a ghost at home, it probably followed her here. And since the smell is gone now, I'm guessing it left with her too."

Why would a ghost come along for a ride to the Haunted Antique Shop? Maybe he wanted to demonstrate his presence in a way that couldn't be mistaken for a coincidence. Maybe he just wanted to be acknowledged. There's also a chance that he was familiar with the shop from the time when it was still a family home. Maybe he knew some of the other spirits in residence, or maybe he was attracted to one of the items we have for sale. Since the ghost was gone, I couldn't ask—and since I'm not a fan of horrible smells, I didn't want to invite him back to find out.

In fact, just to be sure he didn't make a return visit, I cleared the air with cedar smoke and sprinkled the entryways with salt. We might be haunted, but we're only open to ghosts who smell good.

HAUNTED CHARLIE

Whenever you come to the Haunted Antique Shop, you'll find our Haunted Charlie doll stationed somewhere prominently. Sometimes he sits on the fireplace mantel. Sometimes he's positioned on a sideboard in the front room.

Sometimes he keeps watch over the cash register on the checkout desk. He doesn't always move around the shop of his own volition—but I think he could if he wanted to.

Image 11: Our Haunted Charlie doll is the ghostly guardian of the shop.

Charlie is a composition doll, crafted from sawdust and glue mixed with cornstarch or resin. He probably dates back a hundred years, when boy dolls were relatively rare. He's got a serious little face, and sometimes he looks like he's frowning. He might be a subset of little boy dolls that were marketed as "grumpy boys."

At some point in the past, his nose was punched in a little, which only makes him look cuter. His feet are bare, his linen romper is yellowed with age, and there's an old piece of string tied and knotted around his wrist. It might be from an original tag, or it could be an aging remnant of a child's affection.

Dolls are more than simple toys. Whether they're carved from wood, crafted of porcelain or clay, or molded of modern plastic, they are tributes to the human form.

There's also something supernatural about some of them—especially antique dolls, which are older than anyone alive today. They seem wiser, more prescient, and more experienced than their baby faces would appear. I can't tell you how many people come into the shop who love browsing through our displays of regular antiques, but they literally back up or turn around to avoid coming face-to-face with our vintage dolls.

Scientists and researchers say dolls are inherently disturbing—not because they harbor ghosts, but because the human mind doesn't know how to perceive their faces. They look almost human, but they don't blink or breathe or smile. Their perfect stillness triggers a response called the uncanny valley effect. It's a psychological phenomenon: our minds recoil when a lifeless visage looks alive but fails to register as fully human. Throw a few *Chucky* or *Annabelle* movies into the mix, and some people go on to develop a primal fear of dolls. A few even get full-blown phobias.

I admit old dolls are kind of creepy. I understand the uncanny valley effect.

I think there's more to it, though. I think some antique dolls actually do harbor traces of lost lives. Some of our antique dolls have heads of bone china, for example, which is made from the ashes of animal bones. Some of the dolls have real human hair, harvested from the heads of people who haven't walked the earth for two hundred years. Some of the dolls were embraced by children who grew up, grew old, and passed away long before we were born. And when we leave those dolls alone at night, some of them, like Haunted Charlie, move by themselves.

I found Charlie at a swap meet, and ever since I rescued him from a card table filled with beaten-up old toys, he's been a prominent fixture in the shop. After his first night with us, we noticed that his arms move on their own. I regularly position them comfortably on his lap or on the arms of his little wooden chair, but when I come back, they've shifted. They're not falling down due to gravity. He actually raises his arms higher or spreads them wider than I leave them.

When I set up the Cabinet of Curiosities, Charlie was one of the first items to be featured prominently in the display.

Two months later, three customers visited from Boca Raton, which is a few hours away from us, in South Florida. They came into the shop on a Saturday afternoon. One of the first things they did was grab a brochure and start looking at it. One of the women asked, "Why do you call this place haunted?" That's what got them over to the Cabinet of Curiosities.

They chatted for a few minutes, looking at the artifacts in the cabinet. They even introduced themselves. The man's name was Tom, and he was with his girlfriend and another woman, whose husband had died. They said they had been friends for years.

We showed them Charlie, who was seated on a shelf at eye level. "Sometimes his arms move in ways that defy gravity," we explained. "They move up, not down."

They took it all in and kept chatting. We closed the cabinet doors and Tom took a seat in Lucinda's rocking chair. (We assume she moved out of the way first.)

The three visitors said they'd had a few personal encounters, and one of the women pulled out her phone to play a tape she'd recorded. She said it was a ghost talking to Tom, and he nodded in agreement.

Suddenly, everyone heard a clunk coming from the cabinet. It was a pretty loud thunk, as if something had fallen off a shelf. Tom stopped rocking and his eyes got big. "Charlie just turned around," he said. We don't know how he knew; the doors were still closed.

When we opened the cabinet, however, Charlie really was sitting backward. A moment earlier, he had been facing forward, with his chair on the center of a doily. But now he was turned all the way around, facing the back, and the doily was twisted, just as if someone had used their hands to move the chair and spin it with their wrist.

Everyone stared in amazement. One of the women said, "He did turn around!"

Tom didn't wait to see more. He jumped to his feet and sprinted to the door in three long steps. The women followed him out.

Since then, we've had several people take a special interest in Charlie. Those with empathic abilities said they got the distinct impression he didn't like being shut away behind closed doors. I pulled him out and put him on the fireplace mantel.

Image 12: I took this photo right after Charlie turned completely around in the Cabinet of Curiosities. The cabinet doors were closed, and nobody had touched the doll. People standing nearby simply heard a "thunk."

Just before Halloween that year, we held a séance with a mystical study group from DeLand. The organizer, Jo, conducted psychic readings for everyone at the table. When she saw me watching, she remembered Charlie.

"Let's bring him in," she said, smiling. "I've got a feeling Charlie has something he wants to tell us."

She held Charlie in her hands, then set him on the table in front of her.

"It's not that Charlie is inhabited by a ghost," Jo said, "but there is a male spirit in the shop who identifies with Charlie. He would have looked like Charlie as a child. Later, he went to war, and when he came back, he was changed. He was never truly himself after that happened. He drank. And he spent a lot of time in this neighborhood. This house was very familiar to him. His name might actually have been Charlie. So now he's comfortable here. He feels welcomed here. And if you allow him to be of service, he says he'll guard the shop for you."

Who could refuse an offer like that? We happily appointed him to the position he requested.

Before long, we found out that Charlie was true to his word, and he has frightened off at least one would-be thief. That story is next.

UNWANTED COMPANY

We often tell people that our haunted Charlie doll is the unofficial guardian of the shop. We say it with a smile, and most people think it's just lighthearted banter. They even get a little chuckle when they picture the six-inch baby doll as a bouncer.

Image 13: The front room of the Haunted Antique Shop is spooky—but not scary.

Most of them don't realize that we're serious. Dead serious, if you will.

I was alone in the shop on a late spring afternoon. The sun was still high in the sky, and the shop was filled with bright light streaming through century-old windowpanes. Sunbeams danced across the mahogany furniture in the front parlor, and sun rays bounced off the antique mirrors on the wall.

The shop was scheduled to close in five minutes, so I had already started tidying the front room and shutting down for the night.

When the front door opened, I happened to be standing a few feet from the entrance. I found myself face-to-face with a tall, thin, visibly nervous young man. He could have been sixteen. He could have been twenty-six. I couldn't tell, exactly. He wore an oversized hoody that was too warm for Florida weather, which might have explained the beads of sweat on his forehead. His eyes darted back and forth as he looked furtively around the room.

"Hello," I said, trying to gauge how much I should interact with him. "How can I help you today?"

He stiffened, apparently noticing me for the first time.

"Yeah," he said, taking a step back. "You know what? I don't think they want me here."

"What do you mean?" I asked. I was legitimately confused. Did he have friends outside? Was he psychotic? What was I missing? "Who are *they*?" I asked, cautiously.

"The ghosts!" he exclaimed. "The ghosts!"

And with that, he backed away slowly until he was out the door. Then he spun on his heel and ran full speed down the street.

I think that he was "casing the joint," as they say on the cop shows. He was "looking for trouble," as my grandmother would have said. He was up to no good, as I suspected from the start ... but he hadn't counted on Charlie and Company.

In this case, even the suggestion of ghostly guards was enough to send a bad guy on his way.

I could have worried after the fact, but the danger had passed. I looked around, feeling perfectly secure. I visualized the shop safe, sound, and bathed in white light. Then I locked the front door and went home.

THE MISSING GHOSTS

We've got an old lithograph of Andrew Jackson in the shop. It's tucked into a dark corner of the Cabinet of Curiosities, where it's shielded from sunlight and rough handling. The print is practically a museum piece. It's hand-colored, in a handmade frame, and looks like it rolled off the press last year. In reality, the artwork is almost two hundred years old.

Image 14: "Death of General Andrew Jackson," a hand-colored lithograph by Nathaniel Currier, was printed in 1845.

Tinted in tones of burgundy and white, it's a melodramatic depiction of the former president, "Old Hickory," at the moment of his death. As he lies in bed, breathing his last, family members pray and gaze mournfully at his lifeless form.

When people come across the lithograph in our shop, they feel a cold chill run down their spines. Few could say the reason why.

I think I know. If it weren't for Andrew Jackson, our shop probably wouldn't exist. The city of DeLand would never have been founded, and most of Florida would still belong to the Seminole Indians.

When we look at the image of Andrew Jackson, finally meeting his maker, we also sense the spirits of the missing: generations of Native

Americans who lost their land and their lives, and generations more who would never be born.

Native people have lived in Florida for twelve thousand years. Explorer Ponce de León claimed the peninsula for Spain in 1513. The Spaniards founded St. Augustine in 1565; today, it's the oldest city in the United States, just seventy-five miles northeast of DeLand.

Spain's reach never extended much further than St. Augustine, but the Spaniards did manage to wipe out most of Florida's native population. The Indians were killed and captured, died of smallpox, or, later, found themselves sold into slavery in the Caribbean.

In the meantime, British and French settlers were establishing American states and territories to the north. As Europeans claimed more and more land for themselves, some Native Americans fled south to the vacant Florida wilderness—including Central Florida, where DeLand would someday stand. Escaped slaves who fled plantations in the Southern states found refuge with the Seminoles too.

In 1817, Andrew Jackson launched the first of three wars against the slave-harboring Seminoles. The fighting would last for decades.

He started by marching across Florida's international boundaries to settle the "Indian problem." He burned Indian villages and hanged two Englishmen he suspected of inciting the Indians, which created an international crisis.

Then he ignored an 1823 treaty that gave the Seminole people four million acres in Central Florida. The Indians had been promised safety and security, along with twenty years of payments to guarantee the peace. They built towns and planted crops and were well on their way to establishing a new homeland. Instead of abiding by the terms of their agreement, however, US agents spent decades harassing the Indians, demanding that they sell their cattle and pigs to the federal government, and repatriate black members of the tribe to Southern states to be enslaved again.

In 1830, soon after Jackson became president, he instituted the Indian Removal Act. Government agents were merciless. They rounded up the

Seminole people and jammed them onto ships that carried them north, ultimately forcing them to march to Oklahoma on the infamous Trail of Tears.

The Seminoles fought back, of course, with guerilla war techniques that extended the war for decades. Ultimately, a few Seminoles managed to escape to the Everglades in South Florida, and some maintained a foothold in the Tampa area to the east. In the end, however, the Indians were outgunned. The US government sent both its navy and its army after them and wasted approximately fifty million dollars to defeat them.

The true cost of the Seminole Wars boggles the mind. Thousands of lives were lost, and generations more would never be born. What would Florida be like now if Andrew Jackson had left the state and its people alone?

That picture of Jackson on his deathbed? It gives me chills now to think of the millions of people who would have lived—who could have lived—if not for the likes of Andrew Jackson. Their absence is palpable. They are the missing ghosts.

WINSTON CHURCHILL'S TOY

We have something else in the Cabinet of Curiosities from another world leader, and it's a lot more fun than a portrait of a dying president. It's an old cup-and-ball toy that purportedly belonged to Winston Churchill, prime minister of England during World War II. We don't have any paperwork to prove the claim; we bought it from a collector, who said he found it in an antique shop in Europe.

The plaything is a fairly common Victorian-era toy, with an elegant, expensive design. Both the ball and the handle are crafted from walnut. The handle was turned on a lathe, like Queen Anne spindle work. The bottom of the handle is big and round, so when the ball is in the cup, both ends are perfectly symmetrical. It's heavily lacquered, with the right amount of aging and patina for a product of that era.

Image 15: This cup-and-ball toy reportedly belonged to Winston Churchill.

People who hold the toy feel a strong, vibrating energy. It literally makes my hand and arm tingle. The odd thing, however, is that I only notice that sensation when I hold it in my left hand. That prompted me to do a quick online search—and as it turns out, Churchill was left-handed.

We can't prove that the toy once belonged to Churchill. There's no paperwork, no provenance, no proof of any kind. But what if it's true?

RADIO INTERFERENCE

Not all of our ghostly encounters come straight from the Spirit World. Sometimes our customers themselves generate supernatural activity.

Let me set the stage for this story. When we don't have customers, I'm usually in my office writing, working on social media, or planning classes and events. When my daughters come in to help, they're either at the front desk or in the office with me.

We all like a vintage vibe, so during shop hours we usually stream background music on a network of digital devices. We have small speakers strategically hidden throughout the shop, but the primary unit is tucked inside a hollowed-out antique radio cabinet in the front room. When it plays, it sounds like songs from the 1940s and '50s are being broadcast straight from the distant past. It feels like music is being beamed into our own little time warp.

One morning, I was at my desk in the office while my daughter Kate was in the front room. Suddenly, our sound system went haywire. All of our speakers are part of the same networked group, programmed to play the same station at a fairly low volume. Out of the blue, however, they all started playing different songs in every room—loudly. That was bad enough, but then the sound levels started going up and down at random. The volume in the front room rose and fell as if someone was dialing it back and forth by hand. The unit in our tarot parlor started screeching full blast, suddenly reaching a deafening roar.

Image 16: The DeLand Independent Band posed before a performance in the early 1900s.

Just as I stood up to investigate, Kate sounded the alarm. "We've got customers!" she shouted, raising her voice above the clamor. I scrambled, running from room to room to unplug all the speakers and stop the cacophony before the shoppers came in.

It worked. I think we looked calm, cool, and collected as they walked through the door. At that moment, however, we felt the energy shift as if a storm had blown in.

The customers looked like an ordinary mother and her teenage daughter. The daughter was wearing jeans and an astrology t-shirt with a vintage sun and moon woodcut pattern. From the way she was dressed, we figured that stopping by had been the daughter's idea—but it soon became apparent that the mother wasn't fully on board with the idea of psychic phenomena.

As they looked around, the mother criticized her daughter nonstop. "I bet you like *this*," she said sarcastically, pointing to a Haunted Antique Shop mug. "Cabinet of Curiosities?" she sneered. "Yeah, *right*." Her daughter didn't say a word; she just shrugged and kept moving. They made their way through the whole shop, passing from room to room, with the daughter silent and the mother mocking her daughter's interest whenever she stopped to look at anything.

We could only watch in stunned silence as they swept through the shop. Their visit didn't last long, but after they left, Kate and I both let out a deep sigh. Until that point, we didn't even realize we had been holding our breath.

Experts in the paranormal often say that ghosts and spirits can tap into electrical energy to communicate. In this case, however, I think it was the living souls who wreaked havoc with the electronics in our shop. The mother's disrespect clearly changed the emotional energy in the shop. The teenage daughter might also have felt victimized enough to channel her emotions into an electrical vortex, which is practically an open invitation to poltergeist activity.

Some people think poltergeists are ghosts. It's an easy misunderstanding. The word *poltergeist* itself is German for "noisy ghost," and it refers to spirits that make noise or play pranks. Most poltergeist activity, however, comes from living people—especially adolescent girls. It's a form of psychokinesis or telekinetic ability that stems from strong feelings of fear and distress. Emotionally vulnerable people with no other outlet for release can unleash psychokinetic energy—slamming doors, upturning furniture, and making themselves heard the only way they can.

"SHEET" MUSIC

I told you how some of our customers made our sound system go haywire once. Honestly, though, we have ongoing issues with background music in the shop. I think that's because one of our resident spirits has strong opinions about the songs we choose—and all too often, our choices just don't measure up.

Image 17: We sell a range of antique sheet music at the shop. We think of Miss Dennis every time we see it.

Annette Dennis was a music teacher who lived in the house during the 1950s. She might have been affiliated with the university, state college, or public school system. She probably taught piano and voice lessons here too. I can't find any other record of her, except for her listing in the city directories of the time.

Even so, I can picture her clearly in my mind's eye. She has auburn hair with short bangs in front and a French twist in back. She wears a powder-blue sweater set, with reading glasses on a chain around her neck. She spends most of her time in our tarot parlor—until someone tunes our sound system to a station she doesn't like. Miss Dennis had a trained ear, and she still feels territorial about the music she hears in her house.

The Michael Bublé station usually plays without a hitch. She loves the smooth crooner with his swingy jazz stylings. Glenn Miller gets a thumbs-up too because the sound of his big band orchestra is timeless. Frank Sinatra, Ella Fitzgerald, even Dean Martin: all good. Classical music? We could play it night and day.

Sometimes, though, we want to switch things up, especially if we're in the shop after hours and we don't have to stick to a golden oldies theme to set the mood. We'd like to listen to a few top forty songs, maybe some pop music, or even a little classic rock…if only we could. When we switch to anything current or contemporary, the music comes to a screeching halt, and no amount of begging or pleading will get it back.

Miss Dennis has her standards—which means we do too.

TILL DEATH DO US PART

At first glance, Jim and Rosie seem like any other newlywed couple. She's a blushing bride in a silk gown and veil, and he's a handsome groom in a black tuxedo. Both are smiling because the marriage ceremony went smoothly, the reception was a smash, and Rosie's hair is only slightly disarrayed from dancing. Jim has a twinkle in his eye, anticipating still more celebration on the first night of their honeymoon.

The vintage dolls live in the Cabinet of Curiosities, where I'm careful to make sure they both look their best. Every day, when I open the shop, I make sure the groom has his arm wrapped lovingly around his bride.

Most of the time, the dolls stay in position. But every few days, I find them at odds, with Jim's arms at his sides and Rosie facing away, turning her back on her handsome husband. Why? I have a theory.

The dolls are named after James and Rossie Hearne, who lived in the house during the 1930s. James was a dry cleaner. According to old city directories, his shop was a few blocks away, close enough to walk when he needed air.

Image 18: The ghosts of James and Rossie Hearne often toy with the bride and groom dolls in our Cabinet of Curiosities.

Rossie stayed home, but her life was stressful because Mary Hearne, James's widowed mother, lived with them.

Our little bungalow is a charming home, but it wasn't designed to house an extended family. Rossie and Mary would have been in each other's space all day, every day, with no reprieve.

Poor James. When he came home at night, he would have found his mother welcoming her baby boy with open arms—and his wife at her wit's end.

I can imagine Rossie summoning James into their bedroom, where she would unleash all of her anxiety and frustration. James, of course, would defend his mother—the caregiver who raised him and the woman he felt obligated to support in her old age. He'd also vow to smooth things over with his wife and to love and honor her for the rest of his life.

When I started running the Haunted Antique Shop, I sensed discord in the bedroom I use as my office. At first, the energy in the room seemed tense, as if I had inadvertently walked into the middle of an argument. I cleaned the room, physically and psychically, and it turned into a bright and cheerful place to write and work.

When I see the newlywed dolls standing at odds, I'm reminded of those moments of distress. Even so, I can tell they're fleeting.

The ghost of James's mother is long gone, off to join James's father in their own heavenly home. I've tried to contact her without success.

When the older woman died, I think James and Rossie were free to focus on their own relationship and build their marriage into a strong and lasting force. Sometimes I wonder if the dissension I felt in the bedroom was residual, not ongoing. But I do know that James and Rossie still visit on occasion.

I think they move their little counterparts, the Jim and Rosie dolls, as a playful reminder of their presence. Now that their earthly existence has come to an end, they're free to enjoy each other's company on their own terms. And on special nights, when I close the doors and go home, James and Rossie have their old house to themselves.

HEAVENLY HOMES

From what spirits have shown me of the afterlife, they can actually choose to carry on in a heavenly version of the earthly home they loved best. I've seen lakeside cabins, two-story foursquare houses, and tropical huts.

And, as we've experienced at the Haunted Antique Shop, I'm not convinced that those heavenly houses don't overlap with their earthly counterparts—assuming they're still standing.

When I'm at the shop, I often feel as though there's another dimension present all around me. I sense an invisible, parallel version of the same house: the same rooms, the same walls, and the same floors, all in a different time. I can even picture an alternate set of furnishings, window treatments, artwork, wall hangings—and, of course, occupants. If the shop is quiet, empty of customers, and I'm simply lost in thoughts and daydreams, glimpses of the past peek through the veil of the present, parting the curtain of this reality.

THE WHEEL OF FORTUNE

There's a poker carousel in our shop that never fails to set off our EMF meter, suggesting a high level of spirit energy. It's made of vintage Bakelite, a type of plastic designed to look like lacquered wood, with red, white, and blue chips stacked around the sides. It spins like a wheel of fortune, tantalizing and mesmerizing.

Image 19: A vintage poker set at the Haunted Antique Shop hints at the desperate longings of a long-lost gambler.

It has slots for two decks of playing cards. They were empty when I found it, so I filled them with vintage decks, old but still sealed in cellophane wrappers.

The carousel is mostly still these days, and yet, it seems to hum with desperation. "Just one more game," it seems to say. "Just one more game, and my luck will turn. Just one more game, and I can go home with money in my pocket."

I'm not a gambler, but sometimes I feel a strange, powerful urge to break the decks open and try my hand.

All in all, I think the set is safest in the Cabinet of Curiosities, where it won't compel anyone to bet more than they can afford to lose.

THE LETTER OPENER

Antique shops are different than most retail stores. Our stock doesn't come from factories, distributors, or manufacturers. It makes its way into the store from private sellers, estate sales, garage sales, and collectors.

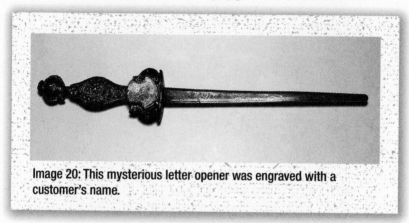

Image 20: This mysterious letter opener was engraved with a customer's name.

Sometimes, I think we get our merchandise from ghosts.

Last spring, I made it my mission to ensure that every single item in the shop was priced and labeled. I thought it would take a day or two. The project wound up taking three weeks.

Until then, I thought I had a pretty good handle on our merchandise. I knew where everything came from, and I thought I knew what it was worth. When customers came in, I was ready with a price. But if I wasn't in the shop, my daughters didn't know what price to ask, which was awkward for everyone. To be honest, I was more than a little embarrassed at all the things I'd put on display without a price tag.

I armed myself with a box of trendy chalkboard tags and a white chalk marker. My handwriting is pretty good, thanks to several years at St. Mary's Academy under the tutelage of Sister Mary Margaret. I wanted our pricing to look sophisticated and comprehensive, and the white-on-black words were dramatic. Ghostly, even.

I started to pull everything off the shelves, piece by piece. As I wrote prices on the tags, I included descriptions of every object, like a museum piece. People like to buy antiques when they know exactly what they're getting.

We had four full rooms of stock to go through. It's all organized by type: kitchenware goes in the kitchen. Fine china and serving pieces go in the dining room. Accent pieces are displayed in the front parlor. You get the idea.

As I neared the end of the big pricing project, I asked my daughter Kate to keep her eyes open and bring me any items I'd overlooked.

One morning, I came into the shop to find a silver letter opener on my desk. "What's this?" I asked her.

"It was in the kitchen," she said, "with the wooden spoons."

I don't think I'd ever seen the letter opener before. If I had, I would have displayed it in the front room on the antique secretary desk next to a vintage paperweight. I might be bad at pricing, but I'm good at organization.

The letter opener was designed to look like a medieval sword, with an ornamental handle and flourishes on the pommel and the guard. I took it over to a window to study it in the bright Florida sunlight. "Look at this," I said. "The blade is inscribed with the name *Jack*."

We both admired it for a minute.

"So where did it really come from?" I asked Kate, teasing her a bit.

"I don't know," she insisted. "It was just there."

A mysterious object of unknown origin? That was enough to land the letter opener in the Cabinet of Curiosities.

In the paranormal world, objects that seem to mysteriously appear and disappear are called *apports*. They're often associated with spirit visits or poltergeist activity. The origin of the word is French; it means "something brought." I like that it also sounds like "teleport."

The letter opener stayed in the Cabinet of Curiosities for a month or two. A few people admired it. Some picked it up and tested its weight in their hands. And then one afternoon a traveling executive came into the shop after a business meeting, looking for a gift to bring home to his wife in Texas. He chose a little porcelain angel for her, a cherub with hand-painted rosy cheeks and gilded wings.

Then he looked inside the cabinet.

"That letter opener," he said, looking at me warily. "It's got my name on it. I mean, it's literally got my name on it. I'm Jack. I've been looking for a letter opener for months, but I wanted to find one that's really special."

"I don't know where it came from," I said, "but it obviously belongs to you."

HERE'S YOUR SIGN

I believe that we can interact with the Spirit World in ordinary ways multiple times a day. You don't need to schedule a reading with a psychic or sit down for a séance or gaze into a crystal ball by moonlight. All you need to do is be open and willing to recognize messages from spirit.

Here's an example.

We have an old-fashioned perpetual calendar in the shop. It's designed like a plaque that can either stand on a desk or hang on a wall. There are three pegs on the front that hold decorative tiles, which you can move around to show the current month and date. It's actually charming and lovely to look at, but for some reason no one has ever wanted to buy it.

Honestly, I get it. Even though the calendar is in our shop, I don't use it myself. I tried, but I didn't always remember to flip the dates every day. Also, when I need to check the date, I'm usually on my phone or at my computer, which is a lot more convenient.

A few months ago, I decided to change the calendar tiles to a random date so my forgetfulness wouldn't be so obvious and no one would mistake it for the current date. I shuffled the tiles around and came up with something totally arbitrary: it was November, so let's say I set the calendar to June 28. Done and dusted, I went on with my regular business.

Image 21: Spirits can communicate through ordinary objects, like this perpetual calendar in our shop.

A day or two later, an older woman came into the shop. She loved everything she saw: the vintage kitchenware, the haunted dollhouse in the parlor, and yes, the perpetual calendar.

"Would you look at that!" she exclaimed. "June 28! That was my mother's birthday! She's gone now, but I think about her all the time."

She kept browsing for a while, then sadly announced that she hadn't found anything she needed to buy that day.

"Not even the calendar?" I asked, ever the hopeful saleswoman.

"No," she sighed. "I don't need a calendar. I guess I was really just hoping for a sign from my mother."

I laughed. "You literally just saw a sign from your mother. It's an actual sign that hangs on the wall!"

She laughed too. She still didn't want the calendar itself, but as she walked out the door, she had a smile on her face.

MAKE ROOM FOR MAGIC

Before any attempt at spirit contact, we ask our customers and clients to make room for magic. We try to spend a few minutes asking them to get comfortable in their chairs, breathe slowly, relax, and open themselves to a mystical experience.

Most are only too happy to try. For many, permission to believe in alternate realities actually comes as a relief.

Granted, it's normal to doubt the reality of supernatural events. We're not raised to believe in the paranormal, and when mystical synchronicities occur, we usually disregard them as mere coincidences. At the Haunted Antique Shop, however, it's okay to set aside your skepticism, suspend your disbelief, and allow miracles to happen.

THE CURSED RING

I used to spend summers with my Grandma Evelyn in Minnesota, in her tiny house on the shores of Lake Minnetonka. She had a jewelry box on her dresser, and she was more than willing to let me try on her necklaces and earrings. She often warned me, however, never to play with the wedding ring in the bottom of the chest. "It's cursed," she said ominously. "It brings nothing but sadness and grief to anyone who wears it."

Years later, after my grandmother died, the ring landed in my own jewelry box. For some reason, no one else in the family wanted it. By then the diamond had come loose, and both the ring and the gemstone were stored in a zip-top plastic bag. For a long time, I kept it like that, imagining that the airtight sandwich bag would keep the curse sealed away.

The ring once belonged to my great-aunt Dolores, whose name, ironically enough, means "Lady of Sorrows." Dolores was my grandfather's baby sister, raised by their widowed mother, mostly in abject poverty.

During the early 1950s, Dolores married a man named Daryl. At first, the family loved him.

"He was so handsome," my mother told me. "He looked like a young Elvis."

Image 22: My aunt Dolores's wedding ring had a long and haunted history.

My grandmother, a professional seamstress, sewed the wedding dress, and my grandfather gave Dolores away.

Daryl and Dolores had five children. And then, tragedy struck, just as it strikes so many couples.

Daryl left his wife and five children for another woman. She was a hairdresser, young, beautiful, and willing to stroke Daryl's handsome head of hair—and his ego.

Dolores was left destitute. She gave her wedding ring to my grandmother, presumably for safekeeping, and went to work for a hatchery, separating day-old female chicks from the males. "Sexing" chickens was—and is—a specialized field. Female pullets are worth more than male cockerels, who tend to fight among themselves, but the visible difference between them is miniscule. Dolores managed to support her family for years that way until her eyes went bad.

Eventually, after I had been running the Haunted Antique Shop for a while, I decided to bring Dolores's ring out of seclusion. I took it to DeLand's Downtown Goldsmith for an assessment.

At first, the jeweler wanted nothing to do with it. "I got this ring from my grandmother," I explained, "and she always said it was cursed."

The jeweler visibly recoiled. "Cursed?" she exclaimed. "Well, I wouldn't know anything about that."

She took a deep breath and gingerly picked up the stone, then studied it under her magnifying loupe.

"Well, it's not a diamond," she said. "It's chipped and scratched, and real diamonds don't show damage like that."

She verified with an electronic gemstone tester and then picked up the ring with the empty mount.

"It looks as though the stone was just glued into place."

"Is the ring itself gold?" I asked.

"Well, it's gold plated. Honestly, I wouldn't even want to clean it. It's just in very poor condition."

Later, she admitted that she didn't even want to touch a ring that was rumored to be cursed.

"Do you hear that rings are cursed very often?"

"No," she said. "Once in a while, but not really."

Another jeweler overheard and joined us at the counter. "If you're just talking about diamonds that were sold after a divorce, you could almost say that all diamonds are cursed. Diamonds get shifted around so much. People are always using and reusing diamonds, and no one really knows where they came from.

"Even so," she said, "if I could wear the Hope Diamond, just for a day, I would. I don't care about curses. I'm all about the jewelry."

Given that I wasn't dealing with a real diamond, used or reused, I decided to take the ring home and repair it myself. I put the stone back in its place with a drop of jeweler's adhesive, and then I called in my aunt, long since passed, for an impromptu spirit reading.

"Aunt Dolores," I asked as I shuffled my tarot deck. "What can you tell me about your ring?"

I pulled two cards from the deck: the Knight of Wands and Death. They seemed to verify the story I'd heard growing up. Daryl *was* handsome and exciting, like the proverbial knight in shining armor, mounted on a racing steed and carrying a torch for the woman he loved. Hot on his heels, however, was Death, the Grim Reaper, slowly marching across a battlefield, striking down anyone who happened to meet his hollow gaze. Clearly, the marriage couldn't survive once the initial flames of passion had died down.

"But was the ring cursed?" I asked.

A third card, the Ace of Cups, told the real story. The Ace of Cups is the card of new love, nourished by a bottomless font of love and devotion, given as a gift from God. And sure enough, by the time I met my aunt Dolores, she was happily remarried to my uncle Elwood.

"The ring wasn't cursed," her spirit whispered. "Daryl was."

JILLIAN'S MIRROR

We like to host small groups of ghost hunters as often as we can. One night, during a full moon, a few of us gathered in the shop's dining room to experiment with dowsing rods.

That evening, a young man named Jon had driven up from Orlando for the gathering. At first, he said he wasn't particularly psychic—but then he started describing the ghostly figures he'd seen all his life. His late aunt, for example, had come to see him shortly after she died. He saw his friend's dead father, fully formed but transparent, walking through a living room and passing through a closed door. And he mentioned, casually, that his own father had been a voodoo practitioner in Central America.

The minute Jon picked up a pair of dowsing rods, they started twitching, as if they couldn't wait to get going. They quivered and shook in his hands, and soon their movements grew stronger and more assured.

"Show me the movement you'll make for 'yes.'" Jon said. The dowsing rods crossed, then uncrossed.

"Show me again," he said.

Image 23: The ghost of a young girl was connected to an antique mirror in our shop.

Again, they crossed and uncrossed in his hands, which he held perfectly still.

"Are you a spirit who'd like to communicate?" Jon asked. The rods crossed in affirmation.

"Are you a man?" They stood still. "Are you a woman?" No response. "Are you a child?" The rods crossed.

"Are you a boy?" Nothing. "Are you a girl?"

The rods crossed, and we all felt a sense of joy and delight fill the room. It felt like she'd been waiting a long time to communicate with us.

We decided to ask her name. Jon started by reciting the letters of the alphabet, hoping we'd reach the first initial. "A ... B ... C ..." he began, but at that point, he stopped.

"I heard 'Jill.'" he said. "The name just popped into my head."

At the exact same moment, I was hit with the impression of *Jillian*. It could have been Jillie Anne, like a mother's nickname for her child, but we all agreed that Jill would work.

"Is there something you'd like to show us, Jill?"

The rods jerked to the right, pointing to the front room.

Jon stood and started walking, following the rods' movement toward the Cabinet of Curiosities.

"Show me what you'd like us to look at."

The rods moved toward a baby doll, positioned in a toy chair, stationed at about eye level. Jon took the doll off the shelf and placed it on a nearby table. Then he smiled.

"She wants to play," he said, laughing. "She wants us to dress the doll."

He confirmed with the rods. They crossed in affirmation.

As luck would have it, I had a bag filled with vintage doll clothes in my office. I riffled through, choosing a hand-crocheted sweater and matching bonnet that were about the right size.

Jon dutifully dressed the doll. Yes, a twenty-something man, in a little antique shop, found himself doing a ghost child's bidding, as if he were a favorite uncle. Once the doll was properly bundled up, we laid her in a toy cradle and put her back on the shelf.

"I feel like there's something else she wants to show us," Jon said. He stood, and the rods pointed toward my office. "It's the mirror," he said, and we all followed him toward a very old, oak-framed mirror that hung behind the door.

By now, Jon was fully engaged in a psychic conversation with the young ghost.

"Are you five, Jill?" The rods crossed in confirmation. "Did you used to live in DeLand?" Yes. "Did this mirror hang in your house?" Yes. "Did your dad use this mirror?" Yes.

Jon looked at the rest of us. "I get the sense that her dad used this mirror to get ready every morning. I can see him standing in front of it, combing his hair and straightening his mustache. Jillian says he was proud of the mirror, and she was proud of how handsome he looked.

"Where did you get this mirror?" he asked me. I told him it had come from a moving sale I happened across, at an old Victorian house a few blocks from the shop.

"Jill," he said, turning back to his new friend. "What happened to you? How did you die? Did you get sick?"

The rods didn't move. "Did you get hurt?" The rods moved toward each other. "Did you get burned?" The rods snapped in his hands, crossing immediately and staying in place.

"She was burned," Jon said, sadly.

"And did your dad try to help you?" The rods crossed and uncrossed. "Is that why you showed us his mirror?" Yes. "Is he with you now?" Yes.

It was all a lot of information to take in. By this point, Jon was starting to feel drained. We'd been practicing for an hour, and talking with a child's spirit can be just as tiring as talking with a living five-year-old. We decided to wrap it up for the night.

"Jill," we said. "Thank you so much for talking with us. We're glad you're okay now, and we're glad you're with your dad. We'll say goodbye for tonight and talk with you again some other day."

HAUNTED MIRRORS

We have several antique mirrors at the Haunted Antique Shop. It's fascinating to imagine all the faces of those who've gazed into those mirrors before us.

There's an old wives' tale that no one should buy a used mirror. Old mirrors, they say, are portals that ghosts can use to travel through time and space. Some believe spirits can glide through the glass to journey between dimensions and cross into this world from the Other Side. Some people even say that if we stand in front of a haunted mirror, gazing at our own reflections, ghosts could mesmerize us and slide into our bodies. Our true selves would be submerged, and a formless spirit could resume his or her physical existence in a stolen form.

I don't doubt that mirrors hold the energy of their former owners, as any object of beauty could. But in my experience, ghosts don't need a special portal to interact with us. They can simply materialize anywhere they wish, without the added effort of passing through glass.

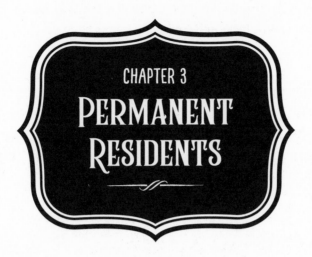

CHAPTER 3

PERMANENT RESIDENTS

B efore DeLand became a city, when settlers first arrived to stake their claims on the Florida frontier, the area was known as Persimmon Hollow. Fruit trees grew wild here, welcoming newcomers with sweet and tangy persimmons the size of plums.

The first house in city limits was a simple log cabin just steps away from the Haunted Antique Shop. It belonged to John and Clara Rich, pioneers who came to carve a new life out of an uninhabited wilderness.

John Rich was a Civil War captain who had come to Florida with the 144th New York Infantry. They didn't come to fight; when they first landed in the state, all the men in his unit were at death's door, and they were sent here to recuperate from the rigors of war.

John was born in Stamford, New York, in 1839. In 1862, at the age of twenty-two, he volunteered for the Union Army. His regiment was dispatched to Washington, DC, and from there, they fought their way south. They were besieged in Virginia, but they turned the tables, and then chased General Lee into Maryland. In South Carolina, they bombarded Fort Sumter and Charleston. And while they were there, every man in the regiment contracted typhoid from contaminated drinking water. Some died. The rest were so ill that their commanders dispatched all of them to a convalescent camp in St. Augustine, Florida—which is where John would have first discovered the promise of the Florida frontier.

Image 24: John and Clara Rich were two of the first settlers in DeLand.
In this photo from 1878, John works in his yard, Clara stands on the porch,
and an African American groom poses next to a horse and buggy.

After the war, Captain Rich went into business in Beaufort, South Carolina. He met and married Clara Fidelia Wright, a New York native whose family had moved there.

In 1875, John and his father-in-law, Cyrenius, staked neighboring claims in Persimmon Hollow. John built a simple cracker house—a one-room log cabin, with a steeply angled roof to shed the rain, an attic for sleeping, and a deep shade porch.

Clara followed them in 1876, along with their two-year-old son, Stephen. John planted orange trees and Clara tended to a huge flock of chickens. A year later, she would give birth to a daughter, Clara Belle, the first child born in DeLand.

The town's first religious service was held in their cabin in 1876. The town's first government was formed there too, when the town council took office in 1882 and Clara's father became the city's first mayor.

When we're alone in the shop on quiet afternoons and the midday traffic comes to a lull, we sometimes hear the sound of horses and wagons passing by on New York Avenue. It's a distinctive noise: the steady clop of the horses' hooves, quiet at first. We don't see the wagon, but the unmistakable sound grows louder as the spectral vehicle draws closer. As it passes directly in front of the shop, we hear the clank of a harness, the squeak of well-worn leather, and the gentle grind of wagon wheels on a gravel road. Sometimes we hear the horses' whinnying, breathing deeply, while a soft male voice urges them forward. After a moment or two, the sound fades away, replaced by the modern hum of cars and the rumble of motorcycles.

Image 25: Captain John Rich, a Civil War veteran, was the first settler to build a home in the future city of DeLand.

We can't be sure, but we think it could be John and Clara Rich, retracing the route they followed so often in life. It seems like a residual haunting, which you'll read about in the next few pages. It's literally the echo of a past event, playing back, repeating on an endless loop through time and space. But if you think about the location of the Haunted Antique Shop, on the main route into DeLand, it's easy to imagine the excitement and anticipation that early travelers would have felt as they approached the pioneer village.

No one felt that energy more keenly than John and Clara Rich, who planted the seeds of a city, nurtured the community, and watched it spring from the earth beneath their feet.

To this day, you'll follow in their footsteps when you walk down streets that bordered their homestead, now named in their honor: Rich Avenue and Clara Avenue. And if you follow Clara Avenue north from their old homestead, you'll find them both on the land they used to own, buried in DeLand's Oakdale Cemetery.

OUR FOUNDING FATHER

We wouldn't be in DeLand if it weren't for one man's dream. The city itself wouldn't have been founded without Henry DeLand, and it wouldn't have survived without his determination to overcome death, despair, and natural disaster.

Image 26: Henry DeLand made a fortune selling baking soda.

Henry DeLand's commitment to his adopted hometown won him lifelong admiration and respect. Unfortunately, it also left him almost penniless.

In the spring of 1876, the millionaire industrialist visited the area for the first time. He came with his brother-in-law, an aspiring investor with "orange fever" who wanted to buy land for citrus groves.

On their first night in Persimmon Hollow, they stayed with John and Clara Rich. Henry was a millionaire, but that night he slept on the rough pine floor of their log cabin. He had a primitive mattress—a bedroll, really—probably stitched together from Civil War Army blankets stuffed with pine needles, then covered with quilts. It was a far cry from the feather-bed he was used to in New York. As he twisted and turned, looking for a sweet spot that would let him drift off to sleep, Henry happened to glance up at the wall. There, through chinks in the stacked logs, he could see stars dancing in an indigo sky.

Image 27: Henry DeLand used collectible trading cards to market his baking soda. He promoted the city of DeLand as enthusiastically as he promoted his business.

He was enchanted. As he continued to gaze out at the night sky, his mind was imagining a future almost too wonderful to believe. Already he was picturing Persimmon Hollow as a center for art, education, culture, and tourism.

The next morning, Henry bought a hundred and sixty acres next to the Rich homestead. He also made plans to come back and buy more land. In fact, he would buy every available parcel in the area.

He returned in the fall, made his land deals, and called all the settlers to a public meeting. As they gathered, once again in John Rich's log cabin, Henry described his vision for a new town.

The settlers loved what they heard—especially when Henry offered to donate land for a school and pay half the cost of the building. He also donated land for a church and a mile-long stretch of land for the town's main street, Woodland Boulevard. He built a hotel and founded the DeLand Academy, which would later become Stetson University.

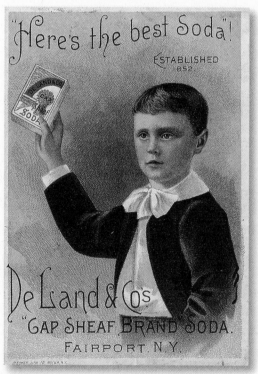

Image 28: The invention of baking soda revolutionized home cooking in the 1800s.

Back in New York State, he had made a fortune selling baking soda and its derivative, baking powder. Today, we take baking powder for granted, but when it was first introduced, it revolutionized the world of home cooking. Without baking soda and baking powder, bread dough was an art most women didn't have time for, and cakes invariably fell flat. When baking soda was introduced, home cooks could successfully whip up their own baked goods in minutes, rather than hours or days.

Henry set to work marketing his new hometown just as enthusiastically as he had promoted baking powder. He advertised his DeLand properties in almost a hundred different newspapers and magazines all over the Northeast and Midwest.

He also guaranteed buyers that if they were unhappy within the first two years, he would buy the land back. That promise would cost him his entire fortune.

Central Florida is subtropical, not tropical. Summers are hot and sunny, and winters are generally mild. That doesn't mean winters are always warm. In December and January, short cold spells snap everyone to attention, with chilly winds at night and frost in the morning.

In the early morning hours of December 29, 1894, the temperature dropped to eighteen degrees. On February 7, 1895, it dropped to nineteen degrees. The cold obliterated acres and acres of young citrus trees. Grove after grove was destroyed. The sap in the fruit trees froze, splitting them open and killing them to the roots. The fruit, shriveled and black, fell to the ground, while dead leaves dangled from lifeless branches.

Before the Great Freeze, Florida had produced six million boxes of fruit per year. After the catastrophe, production plummeted to a hundred thousand boxes. Land lost ninety-nine percent of its value, dropping from a thousand dollars to ten dollars per acre. In other words, Henry DeLand's investment was worthless.

Homesteaders abandoned the area in droves. According to legend, some were so distraught and in such a hurry to leave that they left dirty dishes on their dinner tables.

Heartbroken, Henry DeLand gave up his entire fortune to make good on his promise. He went back to New York and resumed his career in the baking soda industry. He sold his property in Florida, as well as his New York mansion, and the family moved into a modest, middle-class home. He worked until he had paid off all his obligations.

As Henry struggled to rebuild, he faced even greater tragedy. His wife, Sarah, was declared legally insane, a situation no one wanted to talk about. In 1903, their son Harlan died of tuberculosis, leaving a wife and three young children. He was only thirty-seven.

Henry returned to DeLand for a final visit in 1908. By then, the town had rebounded, and he was welcomed like a long-lost friend. At a gathering of the Old Settlers' Society, he described the town's origins so emotionally, there were tears in his eyes. He also said that seeing his old friends was like "a foretaste of heaven." Those words proved to be eerily prophetic. On the way back to New York, his health suddenly failed. Within days he was unconscious, and less than a month later, he was dead.

Later, his nephew Frederick would write that Henry DeLand's life had been a paradox. "He lost everything," he wrote, "but failed in nothing."

Even now, more than a century after his death, Henry DeLand is still a familiar face in the city he founded. The headquarters of the local history center is named in his honor. His photo hangs in shops and restaurants. Most notably, there's a larger-than-life mural of Henry DeLand at a downtown intersection, where he keeps a watchful eye over the city's people as they walk and drive along the main street he laid out in 1876.

And, of course, he's a constant presence at the Haunted Antique Shop, where we have his portrait on prominent display.

ORIGINAL OWNERS

There's an ironic twist to the story of Henry's dream. He came to Central Florida to create a cultural oasis, and he pledged everything he held dear to make his dream a reality.

He started by buying a hundred and sixty acres from two homesteaders who desperately missed the amenities of city life. Mr. and Mrs. Fred Hampson signed the papers, shook hands, and said farewell to Florida.

Shortly after their return to New York, they had tickets for *The Two Orphans* at the Brooklyn Theater. A thousand people packed the auditorium. Behind the stage, a gaslight ignited some scenery. The actors urged calm, but the audience panicked, trampling and jamming the exits. Almost three hundred people, including the Hampsons, were killed

EXIT SIGNS

Astrologers typically work with natal charts, which are calculated for the moment of birth. At the Haunted Antique Shop, I also work with charts from the other end of life: exit charts, cast for the moment of death.

Image 29: An exit chart cast for Henry DeLand's death at four a.m. Friday, March 13, 1908, in Fairport, New York.

I admit that exit charts are unusual. Most astrologers have never heard of them—mostly because I made the term up. The technique isn't taught in books or classes, and it's certainly not traditional. That's because astrologers usually work with charts that point to a life ahead, not a life that has concluded.

I started thinking about exit charts while I was studying for my astrology certification. At first, I called them "death charts." The first time I mentioned "death charts" to other astrologers, they wanted to correct my phrasing. They assumed I was talking about transit or progressed charts, which compare the position of the planets at someone's death to the positions they were at when that person was born.

"No," I tried to explain. "A death chart would be like a birth chart, but it would be a stand-alone chart, cast for the moment of death. We could look at it to see what the soul is taking from this life into the next ... and, maybe, what they'll be focusing on in the afterlife."

Astrologers often study a birth chart for karmic connections to past lives. If we can examine what the soul brings in at birth, there shouldn't be any reason we couldn't look for information about what the soul takes with it at death.

I must have done a terrible job describing the idea, because at that point, the other astrologers looked at me like I had two heads. A few of them shrugged, and then everyone decided to go to the hotel bar.

I stuck with the idea anyway. I never did like the term "death chart," though, because it sounds so final—and death, like birth, is an open doorway to a new life.

As it turns out, exit charts work like a charm. After someone dies, a birth chart doesn't tell their full story anymore. While birth charts describe the promise and possibility of a life in progress, exit charts describe a life well lived. In a sense, an exit chart is a cosmic eulogy. It's a tribute to a soul's experience in this world and its continuing journey into the next world.

An exit chart can also be a source of comfort to those who are left behind, wondering about the onward progression of someone they loved and lost.

Henry DeLand died on Friday the thirteenth in March 1908. His obituary was published in the Rochester *Democrat and Chronicle* the next day—and his exit chart tells his life story from the vantage point of the stars. Here's a brief analysis:

- Rising sign: When Henry died, Capricorn was rising on the eastern horizon. That's a sure sign of business and career success.

- The Sun was in watery Pisces, a sign of spiritual connection. It was also in the second house, where we look for information about wealth and material resources. That's the hallmark of a soul that values wealth because it can enhance spiritual life.

- The Moon was in fiery Leo, which describes Henry's warmhearted, loving personality. It accentuates his flair for drama, which he used to market both his baking soda and the city he founded. The Moon was in the seventh house, where it reflected his desire to build long-lasting partnerships that would benefit others.

- Mercury, the planet of thought and communication, was in Pisces, the watery sign of dreams and escapism. Henry did cast a spell of glamour over his work. His advertisements depicted cherubic children and painted idealized portraits of a picture-perfect home life. And with Mercury in the first house of self, Henry always thought of himself as an advertising man.

- Venus and Mars were both in Taurus, the earthy sign of comfort and tradition. They were both in the third house of thought and communication too. Henry loved the finer things in life, and he was determined to share them with others by establishing a cultural community—DeLand, the Athens of Florida.

- Jupiter, the expansive planet of luck and good fortune, was in fiery Leo, which suggests ostentatious gifts and over-the-top bequests. Henry was a generous benefactor. He didn't simply fund the occasional charity: he built entire churches, colleges, and courthouses.

- Saturn, the ringed planet of boundaries, limitations, and restrictions, was in Pisces, the watery sign of intuition. Henry empathized and sympathized with others, even to his own detriment.

- Uranus, the planet of revolution, was in Capricorn, the sign of business and career success. It was also in the twelfth house of hidden secrets and potential downfalls. Henry was incredibly successful. Unfortunately, the twelfth-house placement also hinted at unexpected disasters, like cold snaps, that would overturn his finances.

- Neptune, the vaporous planet of dreams and illusions, was in watery Cancer, the sign of home and family life. It was also in the sixth house of work and service to others. He made a fortune by selling the dream of home cooking and baking to women across the country.

- Pluto, the planet of unavoidable change, was in Gemini, the sign of communication and curiosity. It was in the fifth house, where we look for information about recreation and play. The gifts he gave, designed to promote a cultural community, grew his fame and fortune—which changed, literally, with the uncontrollable forces of weather.

Twenty years after Henry's death, Helen DeLand wrote her memoirs of the town's founding. In her book, *The Story of DeLand and Lake Helen Florida*, she describes how her father faced his problems head-on:

Some one else must tell how this victory was wrought from defeat. We were involved inextricably in the widespread calamity.... It broke him financially, but his spirit was invincible. He said, "I will begin again. I am sixty years young, not old." So up the way down which he had gone first in holiday mood and afterward had passed and repassed with high hopes, he went, sad, worn, poor, but unconquered.

THE PHILANTHROPIST

When Henry DeLand lost his fortune, the DeLand Academy needed a benefactor. That's when John Stetson, the inventor of the cowboy hat, rode to the rescue.

Image 30: John Stetson made the cowboy hat an icon of American style.

Stetson was one of the richest men in the world. When he came to DeLand, fame and fortune followed. He built a Gilded Age mansion on the edge of town, where royalty and heads of state came to call. He summoned inventors and entrepreneurs like Thomas Edison to boost the city's infrastructure—which meant that DeLand was the first city in Florida to get electricity and an ice plant.

But as John Stetson reached the end of his life, a scandal at Stetson University was brewing. The turmoil divided both the campus and the community, and the men who used to sing John Stetson's praises turned into a pack of jackals.

Ultimately, the scandal left Stetson feeling betrayed and broken. It might even have led directly to his death. While John Stetson's spirit is still a part of the school's living history, his ghost also haunts the shadows of the past.

John Stetson was born in 1830, the seventh of twelve children in New Jersey. His father had been a hatmaker, and as a young man he worked for the family business. In his twenties, however, he contracted tuberculosis. In those days, "consumption" was practically a death sentence. Wracked by a vicious, hacking cough, sufferers would waste away, consumed by a disease for which there was no cure.

Facing certain doom, John Stetson decided to make the most of whatever time he had left. He put the East Coast behind and headed for the clean, open air of America's Wild West.

In 1862, Stetson found himself prospecting for gold on Pike's Peak, Colorado. The weather was cold and wet, and Stetson and his fellow adventurers needed blankets and tents. They had plenty of beaver pelts, but no way to tan the hides. That's when Stetson turned to felting, a process he had learned from his father. While the other prospectors watched in amazement, Stetson shaved the pelts, shredded the fur, and used boiling water to mat the fibers together. Once that was done, they had strong, waterproof felt for tarps and canopies.

Stetson also had enough leftover felt for a hat.

By the fashion standards of the times, the hat he designed looked ridiculous. Back then, men wore close-fitting bowler or derby hats with small brims. Stetson's hat, on the other hand, was huge. Like a ten-gallon hat, it featured an oversized crown and a broad, sombrero-style brim—but it kept him cool in the heat, warm in the cold, and dry in the rain.

When a passing cowboy bought the hat right off his head for a five-dollar gold piece, Stetson knew he was onto something. He went home, borrowed money from his sister, and in 1865 he opened his own hat-making shop in Philadelphia. He was thirty-five.

Stetson was just as bold in business as he had been on Pike's Peak. He hired traveling salesmen to fan out across the country, which was an innovative new way of marketing. They carried small-scale replicas of the hats, which was also a clever new way to showcase their whole product line. Before long, Stetson could hardly meet the demand for his hats. He built a six-story factory and hired thousands of workers. Eventually, they made eleven thousand hats a day, and Stetson made more money than he could count.

I don't know where John Stetson met Henry DeLand. They might have been introduced at a swanky New York soiree or in Florida, where the rich and famous relaxed at oceanfront resorts. Either way, the two men became fast friends.

After the freeze of 1885, when Henry DeLand lost his fortune, he turned to John Stetson for help with his school. Mr. Stetson was all in. Between 1886 and 1906, he donated a million dollars to DeLand Academy. He was so generous with his time and treasure that before long, trustees changed the name to Stetson University. Henry DeLand enthusiastically supported the move. After all, he still had the entire city named in his honor.

Mr. Stetson made the city of DeLand his second home. He brought his young wife, Elizabeth, along with their three sons, to spend every winter in DeLand. Like so many other settlers, he planted orange groves. He also built a power plant, an ice-making factory, a packing plant, and a railroad spur. You know, the usual improvements one makes in a new home. He bought a hotel from Henry DeLand's brother-in-law and proceeded to transform it into a showplace.

Stetson University was always one of his highest priorities. When Mr. Stetson was in DeLand, he visited the campus almost every day, starting with a morning prayer service in the chapel he had built. He paid for several buildings and furnished them too. He funded science labs and pianos for music students. He invited noted lecturers to campus and offered his own business advice and acumen to administrators. He built a house for John Forbes, the young president of the school, and paid his salary too. And if that wasn't enough, he paid for landscaping and firewood, delivered crates of oranges to hungry students, and invited faculty and staff to dinners at his home and gave them Christmas gifts.

Given Mr. Stetson's generosity, it's hard to imagine how the school's leadership turned on him in his final days. Maybe their visits to his mansion swelled their heads. Maybe their relationship with a man of immense wealth convinced them all they were more important than they truly were. Maybe they were jealous. At any rate, their admiration would come to a bitter end. The recipients of all his donations and largesse turned on him in a shocking courtroom-style showdown.

THE FORBES SCANDAL AND THE DEATH OF HENRY STETSON

John F. Forbes was just thirty-two when he signed on as president of the new DeLand Academy in 1885. He was a competent administrator, and the school grew steadily under his guidance.

He had help, of course, from Mr. Stetson, who mentored him. The two men strategized often, and at one point, John Forbes said the older man was like a father to him.

That ended during the summer of 1901, when the university hosted a special series of continuing education classes for public school teachers. Normally, Forbes and his wife, Ida, would have gone to their summer home in New York. That year, however, Forbes decided to stay in DeLand and teach at the summer session.

That's when the rumors started—because Forbes wasn't staying home alone. He was spending most of his time with Lena Mathes, a charming, thirty-something education professor from Tampa. Lena was married, but her husband was in his sixties, and he was still on the west coast of Florida.

That summer, John and Lena were practically inseparable. They took long buggy rides together, across the campus and around the town. When she wasn't teaching, she would spend hours with him in his office, behind a door that stayed firmly closed. At night, he would visit her, too, in her dorm room in Chaudoin Hall. He was even seen climbing in and out of her window when he thought no one was looking.

Image 31: John Forbes, the first president of Stetson University, was embroiled in a scandal that nearly destroyed the school's relationship with its most important donor, John Stetson.

You read that correctly. The president of the university was climbing in and out of a dorm room window, presumably to avoid a matron, who kept a close eye on the young women in her care.

It was a scandal, and the affair rocked the campus. Some students and teachers even threatened to leave, until Lena Mathes suddenly left the school herself—reportedly due to an undisclosed illness. That led to even more speculation: some said she'd lost a pregnancy and that bloody evidence had been discovered in a closet in or near her room. Rumors flew all over town, all whispered in tones of shock and alarm.

As school resumed that fall, and Lena Mathes stayed in Tampa, the rumors receded. The scandal had almost died down when Forbes announced that Lena was coming back—and he demanded that the faculty receive her with kindness and respect.

That was a step too far. Stetson was a Baptist school, after all. Several professors went to Mr. Stetson, complaining about the situation and threatening to resign.

Mr. Stetson was shocked. He couldn't believe that John Forbes, the son of a Baptist minister, would betray his wife, his family, or their work together. He didn't want to believe that Forbes could be so reckless.

As more staff and students talked about leaving the school, Mr. Stetson knew he had to act. He came up with a plan that he thought would clear up the whole situation without destroying anyone's reputation or hurting the university.

In February 1902, he held a series of private hearings at his luxury hotel, the College Arms. John Forbes and Lena Mathes both testified, and both proclaimed their innocence. But a string of others came in with eyewitness accounts of Forbes and Mathes's affair. They all told the same story over and over again, until Mr. Stetson was convinced that the rumors were true. At the end of the day, Mr. Stetson asked Forbes for his resignation. He tried to ease him out with dignity, by offering a year-long leave of absence with a full salary.

Forbes said he'd have to think about it. He headed off to New York, where his twin brother George convinced him to go back to Florida and fight for his job and his honor.

Forbes started contacting trustees in secret, saying that he was being slandered. He painted Mr. Stetson out to be a power-hungry tyrant who wanted the university under his complete control. He convinced the board that Mr. Stetson wasn't acting out of goodwill, but out of a crazed lust for power.

Mr. Stetson wasn't tuned in to the subterfuge that was taking place behind his back. Instead, he was focused on getting to the bottom of the Forbes affair. He hired an attorney, Isaac Stewart, to investigate.

That fall, Mr. Stetson called a meeting of the school's trustees. The meeting that resulted was excruciatingly long. It lasted from seven p.m. to one a.m. the first night and from eight a.m. to six p.m. on the second day.

It took more than four hours to read the sworn statements the lawyer had gathered. They all told the same story, and John Forbes and Lena Mathes looked guilty as sin.

But the attorney overplayed his hand by including testimony from a man who had been in charge of the school's dining facilities. Forbes had fired him, conveniently enough, on charges that he had stolen, beaten his wife, and used obscene language. Looking back on it now, Forbes could have fired the guy for any one of those offenses, but this was part of a master plan. Forbes wanted to make the cafeteria employee look like a total scoundrel so he would be entirely discredited.

Forbes had already primed the board to presume the worst about Mr. Stetson's charges. He warned them ahead of time that Mr. Stetson was trying to run the school like a dictator, using his fame and fortune to deprive them of their status and authority. When they finally heard evidence from an apparently untrustworthy source, they decided to seize it as an excuse to punish Mr. Stetson for making them all feel small. They turned on Mr. Stetson and accused him to his face of using his wealth to dig up dirt on an innocent man.

After the meeting, John Forbes described the ongoing assault in a long, blustering letter to his brother—and if anyone sounds like a power-mad tyrant, it was Forbes.

"We began the defense," he wrote, "But I was no longer on trial: *he* was on trial...Stetson saw doom coming, and he then made a pitiful plea, as I say, through his men, for mercy."

Forbes even criticized Henry DeLand, who had come from New York for the meeting. "DeLand made one of his whining, bragging, sentimental speeches that came pretty nearly driving everyone out of the room with nausea." What had the old man said that made Forbes so sick to his stomach? Only that he loved the university, feared for its future, and believed that John Stetson was a good man.

Forbes was gleeful as he told his brother how one of the trustees, William Chaudoin, had condemned Mr. Stetson outright. The old man was near death and so feeble he had to lie on a couch during the long proceedings, but afterward he rose to proclaim John Forbes's innocence.

"He said there was a Just and Righteous God in Heaven, and in as much as Stetson had been willing to break the heart of my wife, and ruin my children, the Judgment of God would certainly come upon him, upon his purse and upon his family."

It sounds suspiciously like a curse—and John Forbes was more than pleased with the result.

"By lifting my finger," he wrote, "I could have absolutely ruined him by the verdict of the Board of Trustees. They had drawn up resolutions blazing hot against him, but I induced them to cut them out for my sake. There never was a greater battle, or greater victory. But I have said enough about myself. The sky is bright now. The prospect is for the greatest year of the University in its history. We are all well, and the relief is simply inexpressible."

That relief was short-lived. Lawsuits followed on all sides, along with accusations of slander and libel. Before long, the trustees took their condemnation of Mr. Stetson one step further and voted to remove him as president of the board.

Not surprisingly, Mr. Stetson quit giving money to the school, and the university started going into the red.

Forbes stayed on as president of the school, but he'd lost the respect of faculty, staff, and students. Before long, he realized that his reputation had been destroyed. He took a leave of absence, then resigned. He went back to Rochester, New York, where he bought a business school.

A new president, Lincoln Hulley, took office. He reached out to Mr. Stetson, hoping to reconcile, and hoping that Stetson would start writing checks again. Sure enough, Mr. Stetson stepped up and paid off the school's most outstanding debts.

But Mr. Stetson hadn't forgotten how terribly the board of trustees had treated him. In fact, he offered to donate a hundred thousand dollars to the school if the old board of trustees would resign.

When they refused, Mr. Stetson retreated to his mansion. He wasn't a young man. He was seventy-five, and he felt it. The stress and strain of battling with the school he had loved had taken its toll. Three days after that final meeting with the board of trustees, he suffered a stroke, collapsed, and died as he was preparing for a bath on the second floor.

It was a sad, ignominious end to a life of service and success.

CHAPTER 4
NEIGHBORHOOD HAUNTS

DeLand has more than its share of ghosts, which means the Haunted Antique Shop has plenty of spectral neighbors. For years, people have reported ghostly activity at a number of nearby locations.

The most famous neighborhood haunt is John Stetson's former home, about a mile from our shop. Because it's so close, I happen to drive by it a few times a week. It's not on a main thoroughfare, though, so you probably won't see it unless you seek it out. Like all of the haunted hot spots in this book, its doors are often open to the public—and it's well worth a special trip.

After Mr. Stetson died, his wife, Elizabeth, closed up the mansion and returned to Pennsylvania to bury her husband. For years, the DeLand estate sat empty, with only a caretaker to manage it.

Today, the grounds of the Stetson Mansion are a pass-through for lighter, brighter spirits, who visit to relive the parties and soirees that used to spill out from the mansion onto the expansive lawn. Walk past at twilight and the early evening hours, and you can see glittering orbs and sparks of light dancing through the gardens. You might even hear strains of old songs, echoes of the musicians who played outdoor concerts in the yard.

Image 32: The Stetson Mansion, shown here in 1890, has been fully restored to its Gilded Age glory. While it's still a private home, it's frequently open for public tours.

Inside, some guests have reported paranormal activity in the middle bedroom on the second floor. One woman reported that she was kissed while she slept there. A former owner saw ghostly ectoplasms going up the grand staircase and often struggled with spirits who took over the electrical system and controlled television remotes and the lights on the third floor. Another visitor drew a picture of a nineteenth-century servant she saw in the parlor.

The Stetson Mansion has always been a stately home, complete with rounded bays and towers. It had been designed as a luxury retreat, where the Stetsons could escape the northern cold for the comfort of a Florida winter. Originally, John had planned to build a sprawling mansion. When his wife reminded him that it was merely their winter cottage, he kept the finished design down to three stories with ten thousand feet of living space. He reportedly invited Louis C. Tiffany, the stained-glass master, to design his windows, and he called on his friend Thomas Edison to oversee the electrical work. You can still see Edison's handwritten notes on the original electrical panel near the kitchen. Edison also helped Stetson set up the first power plant in the area, making the city of DeLand the first town in Florida to have electricity.

As visitors followed the winding drive through wrought iron gates, they once passed through a phalanx of exotic peacocks, strutting like elegant sentries across the manicured lawn. As they drew closer, they would have gazed at the Tiffany windows, with ten-thousand panes of leaded glass, all sparkling like diamonds. And as they crossed the threshold through the oversized front double doors, they would have felt as if they were entering a cathedral, with a stunning grand staircase, parquet floors, and a glass wall imported from a French chateau.

The Stetsons' DeLand home had been designed to entertain and impress the highest echelons of society. Between 1887 and 1906, John and Elizabeth welcomed a global array of the rich and famous, including President Grover Cleveland, General Ulysses S. Grant, and King Edward VII, who was then the Prince of Wales. They also hosted some of the world's wealthiest, most powerful couples, like the Astors, Carnegies, Mellons, and Vanderbilts.

After Mr. Stetson died, the house stayed in the family, but it sat vacant for almost twenty years. In 1925, most of the land around the mansion was sold and divided into residential lots. Over the years, the mansion itself has gone through many owners. It's been used as a tearoom, bed and breakfast, restaurant, museum, music studio, and piano school.

It was completely renovated and restored to showroom status in 2008. It's still a private home, often open for tours by appointment.

ON LOCATION: THE GATOR PIT

The Stetson Mansion is located at 1031 Camphor Lane, DeLand. Stetson's alligator pond is behind the mansion. You can see it from West Voorhis Avenue.

When John Stetson welcomed his guests, he often treated them to a sight they could only see in Florida: his pet alligator, Beauregard, who lived in a concrete pond behind the mansion.

Alligator Pit Was Curiosity

Image 33a: John Stetson, his wife, and two of their guests watch a keeper feed Beauregard, their pet alligator.

Image 33b: Beauregard at the fence.

Image 33c: Beauregard resting.

Image 33d: The pond as it looks now.

Mr. Stetson and his visitors would all troop out to see him. Dressed in their finest, the women holding parasols, the men in dark suits and Stetson hats, they would all stroll across the grounds to see the leathery green creature sunning himself like an ancient dinosaur. For a special treat, Mr. Stetson would ask Beauregard's keeper to hold his feedings until they had an audience. Then everyone would gasp in amazement as the gator's jaws opened wide and clamped down on live fish and raw chickens.

The gator pit is still there, visible from the street behind the Stetson mansion. Simply drive around the block to West Voorhis Avenue and say hello to the gator's ghost.

OUT OF THE ASHES

DeLand doesn't have a town square, but it does have the next best thing: a town center. You'll find it at the intersection of the two biggest streets in the city: Woodland Boulevard and New York Avenue.

Image 34: Charles Miller was the first to rebuild his store after a fire destroyed DeLand's business district in 1886.

This is where Henry DeLand first staked his claim in a forest of yellow pines, then carved primitive roadways through the sandy soil. This is where homes and businesses sprouted, families walked along shaded lanes, and horses pulled wagons tirelessly back and forth.

It's also where the ghost of a one-armed man paces frantically, desperate to clear his name and reclaim his reputation. While most people remember him only as the owner of the Wilcox saloon, his full name was Crawford Peter Wilcox.

Today, the downtown business district could be a movie set. Most of the shops look just like they did a century ago, with inviting window displays, colorful awnings, and benches and flowerbeds along the sidewalks.

Image 35: Woodland Boulevard after the Great Fire of 1886.

But if you close your eyes, quiet your mind, and breathe deeply, you might be transported back a hundred and fifty years. You'll find yourself in a time when the town was little more than a collection of ramshackle structures surrounded by orange groves and one unlucky breeze could blow it all away.

In fact, if you were to stand at that intersection at twilight, with the moon rising over your shoulder, you might even smell smoke from a distant fire—an inferno that roared through this intersection on September 27, 1886.

That night, at two a.m., almost everyone in town was sound asleep. It was a quiet night, so they slept peacefully on featherbeds and mattresses stuffed with soft pine needles, under light woolen blankets or hand-sewn patchwork quilts. Their windows were open, and a gentle, cooling breeze ruffled the lace curtains in their rooms. Throughout the nearby countryside, crickets chirped, frogs croaked, and barred owls called softly in the pines.

Suddenly, there was an eerie moment of silence. For one brief flicker of time, everything stopped. There was no sound, no motion, no breath of fresh air—and then all hell broke loose.

At that instant, everyone in town woke to a living nightmare. The business district was on fire. Red and orange flames illuminated the night sky, casting a strange artificial daylight through the darkness. Columns of white smoke rose toward the stars, while constellations of burning embers spiraled in every direction, setting new fires wherever they landed. Dogs barked, and the horses in Charles Miller's livery whinnied and bucked in a panicked frenzy. "Fire!" someone shouted. "Fire! Fire!"

In the streets, more people spread the alarm—yelling, blowing whistles, and shooting guns. As stable hands led horses to safety, every man, woman, and child who could hold a bucket of water joined the brigade. Volunteer firefighters wheeled in two 30-gallon chemical engines, which were like oversized fire extinguishers on wheels. They were immediately overwhelmed.

City leaders made the difficult decision to let the central business district burn. Most of the buildings in a two-block area were already engulfed. They had been built of dried pine from surrounding forests, and they went up like kindling. As those buildings crumbled and fell, everyone focused on structures that hadn't yet caught fire, draping them in wet blankets, and dousing embers where they landed.

Henry DeLand's daughter Helen was there. Years later, she described how residents saved Dreka's hotel and department store. "They hung wet blankets from the verandahs, then enveloped themselves in blankets, they went up and down to a tank on the roof for water which they kept pouring on the flames, whenever they blazed up. As the men became exhausted, others took their places, until the fire sank into ashes."

In just two hours, twenty-two buildings burned to the ground, and thirty-three businesses were lost. Luckily, no one died, and there are no reports of serious injuries, either.

No serious injuries, unless you count the devastated reputation of one man.

For years, people theorized that the fire had started in the Wilcox Saloon, where Crawford Peter Wilcox ran a billiard hall and sold whisky and cigars. He had boasted that his establishment was clean and sanitary, thanks to the sawdust he used on the floor to catch spills. It would be so easy, everyone said, for someone to leave a cigar unattended and set the whole town on fire.

I'm not so sure about that. Do cigar smokers routinely drop their bad habits in a pile of sawdust and walk away? It's far more likely that a kerosene lantern was left unattended.

Today, the location is home to a series of small shops. It's a bustling stretch of main street, crowded with people who are window shopping, meeting friends, and waiting for a table at one of several restaurants and cafés. But when I took time to visit the place where Wilcox's saloon once stood, I noticed there's a quiet alcove tucked back from the busy sidewalk. It was a Friday night, around eight p.m., and strangely enough, I felt completely separate from everyone else walking by—almost as if I was in a bubble of time and space. I could sense Wilcox's troubled spirit there. I reached out psychically to ask him what actually happened that night. And then, in an ironic twist, a series of fire trucks and police cars raced past, bursting that bubble with flashing lights and sirens blaring. Sometimes, spirits are surprisingly literal in their response to questions.

The truth is that no one really knows how or where the fire started. Wilcox was the fall guy, though, and the fire destroyed more than his business investment. It also destroyed his life. He was only forty-nine at the time, with a wife and four children.

After the fire, his health spiraled downward, and he died three years later. According to his obituary, he'd suffered a host of health problems at the end of his life. He lost his right arm and nearly lost his eyesight.

It's possible that the fire and the humiliation of blame triggered terrible memories of his own past. Twenty-five years earlier, he had enlisted in the

Southern Confederacy. He was wounded in the first big battle of the Civil War, Bull Run, fighting alongside Stonewall Jackson.

After the fire, the city banned wood-frame buildings in its business district. New construction had to be brick or stone. And just for good measure, the council banned saloons too.

THE MILLER-FISH BUILDING

Charles Miller, who lost his livery that night, was the first businessman to rebuild. He commissioned a two-story brick structure, with Italianate details like arched windows and decorative cornices under the eaves. High above the street, on the roof above the door, Miller crowned his new building with a triangular pediment and posted his name prominently along the front. Years later, when Bert Fish bought the building, he would replace Miller's name with his own.

For the next twenty-six years, he sold farm goods, specializing in hardware, hay, grain, and fertilizers. He also served as the agent for the Clyde steamboat line. If you needed tickets to Boston, New York, or Philadelphia, you could buy them from Mr. Miller and soon find yourself sailing up the St. Johns River toward Jacksonville, Charleston, and all points north. Curious about Cuba? You could buy tickets headed south toward the Keys and the tropics too. If long-distance travel wasn't your thing, he would also sell you tickets for day trips on the river so you could enjoy the scenery or visit friends in nearby settlements.

Trains eliminated steamboats, and cars replaced trains, and by the time Charles Miller was ready to retire, most farmers didn't buy their supplies downtown. In 1930, Bert Fish bought the whole corner block and remodeled it. Later, it became a men's shop and then a five-and-dime department store, where many items cost a nickel or a dime—the equivalent of today's dollar stores.

Today, the building looks just like it did when Charles Miller opened his doors in 1887. The Museum of Art—DeLand runs a museum store on the ground floor, along with art galleries and event space upstairs. It's also the headquarters of the MainStreet DeLand Association, which promotes businesses in DeLand's downtown.

While most of the buildings here are historic; there's something special and unique about this particular intersection. It's a liminal space, a gateway between the future and the past, that invites us to step between worlds. And while we stand here, contemplating our direction, both the past and the present hold equal fascination.

ON LOCATION: WOODLAND AND NEW YORK

The intersection of Woodland Boulevard and New York Avenue, DeLand

Image 36: The old Dreka's Department Store at the intersection of Woodland Boulevard and New York Avenue, DeLand.

When you face west at the intersection of Woodland and New York, you'll have a clear view of the Fish-Miller building. Face east, and you'll see the old Dreka's Department Store too. Helen DeLand described how the original structure on the site was saved from the fire. Later, that building was moved down the street, and the current one was built in its place. For years, the Dreka store was the biggest, most respected store in West Volusia County.

Today, it's a restaurant and a bar, because city officials made saloons legal again when Prohibition was rescinded in the 1930s. You can sit back, raise a glass, and commune with the spirits of Mr. Wilcox, Mr. Miller, and Mr. Dreka—three DeLand businessmen who deserve to be remembered.

ENCORE PERFORMANCES

From his first night in Central Florida, Henry DeLand hoped that his city would someday be a center for music, art, and culture. Today, the Athens Theatre is a living monument to Henry DeLand's dream. It lights up the night and serves as a beacon for residents and visitors alike. Once decrepit but now fully restored, the Italian Renaissance building is a downtown landmark.

Image 37: Once abandoned and left in ruins, the Athens Theatre has been restored to its former glory.

It's also the afterlife playhouse of two pioneer children who used to live on the site.

The Athens first opened its doors on January 6, 1922. At that time, Warren G. Harding was president. Rudolph Valentino was starring in a silent movie called *The Sheik*. Another movie star, Fatty Arbuckle, was on trial for murdering a Hollywood starlet. Coco Chanel had just introduced her signature scent, Chanel No. 5, and Albert Einstein had recently been awarded a Nobel Prize in physics. Radio broadcasting was new, and while radio stations were popping up all over the country, hardly anyone actually had a radio receiver in their home.

On that Friday night, the program featured a four-act comic play, four vaudeville acts, and a silent movie, a melodrama called *The Black Panther's Cub*. Some even say a young W. C. Fields was one of the vaudevillians who appeared at the opening.

For years, the theater continued to showcase vaudeville acts and silent movies, accompanied by a Wurlitzer pipe organ. During the Great Depression, the Athens was affordable even when money was tight. When talkies took over, it became a standard movie theater. As the decades unfolded, it also housed a dinner theater and a restaurant.

Over the years, however, the building deteriorated. Stripped of its art deco features, it truly was a shell of its former self, and it closed in the early 1990s.

It sat crumbling and vacant for almost twenty years, until community leaders decided to reclaim the landmark. They restored it to its former glory and reopened in 2009. Today, the theater houses live productions, concerts, dance performances, and the occasional movie, for old times' sake.

The theater also houses regular appearances from ghosts and spirits.

Local legend says a former stagehand haunts the catwalk and the tech bay. Some cast and crew members have seen glimpses of past performers in the dressing rooms and phantom audiences in the empty auditorium.

The Athens's most frequent visitors, however, are Isaac and Maria, a brother and sister who make regular appearances during rehearsals and productions alike. Alexa Baldwin, the theater's executive director, says they seem to be about seven or eight years old.

Baldwin says the children are part of the Athens family. "When we walk in," she said, "we always say hi."

Some theater employees, like facilities manager Alan Ware, have seen Maria's ghost. They describe her as a typical little girl with ribbons in her hair and a simple dress. Others have heard the siblings loud and clear. During a production of *Jekyll & Hyde*, a musical, the entire cast was onstage when they heard both children singing along in the wings.

Image 38: It's possible that Isaac and Maria were included in this photo of DeLand schoolchildren from the 1880s.

"They're mischievous," Baldwin said, "but they don't hurt anything. There is literally no harm to anything they've done. They just like to play."

Isaac and Maria typically like to frolic in the fancy box seats on the left side of the theater. They also run up and down the stairs that lead to the basement dressing rooms and storage areas. They open and close doors, dart across the stage during setup and rehearsals, and tinker with lights and sound equipment. When cast and crew members discover their antics, she said, they also hear the children laughing.

They also get more active the later anyone stays at the theater. When the cast and crew work past midnight, Isaac and Maria get more and more boisterous. "It's almost as though they're saying, 'Hey, it's our turn,'" Baldwin said.

Two teams of psychic investigators, working independently of each other, both reported encounters with Isaac and Maria. They called them by the same names, even though they weren't working together. They also reported the same cause of death.

"They haunt the theater," Baldwin said, "because they died in the livery before the theater was built," she said.

Image 39: Cannon's Livery Stable once stood on the current site of the Athens Theatre.

Cannon's Livery Stable was a fixture at the site for many years, when horses were an essential component of everyday life.

DeLand, like most towns in the late 1800s, was dotted with livery stables, all within walking distance of homes, hotels, and businesses. Livery owners catered to people who didn't have barns or stables of their own, as well as travelers who arrived by steamboat and train. People could board their own horses or rent the livery's. They could even hire livery employees when they needed strong men for moving and delivery; the stables had freight wagons and willing workers. Sadly, livery wagons were routinely called into service as hearses to carry caskets too.

While there's no historical record of a fire at the livery, it's possible that Isaac and Maria were victims of an accidental, fire-related death. In the days before electricity, when cooking and heating both relied on open flame, burns were an ever-present threat. What's more, the DeLand Fire Department also boarded their horses at Cannon's Livery. Perhaps Isaac and Maria were killed elsewhere and simply hitched a ride home with the firefighters who tried to save them.

ON LOCATION: THE ATHENS THEATRE

124 North Florida Avenue, DeLand

The Athens Theatre always has a full production lineup of plays, musicals, and concerts. With 245 seats on the main floor and 206 in the balcony, you can see the stage clearly from any seat in the house.

Book your tickets online or at the old-school box office in front of the theater. Get there early, grab a drink and a snack at the concession stand, and follow along as an usher shows you to your seat.

Settle in and let the historic theater transport you to another time and place. Close your eyes, and you'll hear the same sounds you would have heard at any point in the past: other patrons taking their places, the hushed murmur of the crowd waiting for the curtain to rise, and the occasional clatter of a stagehand placing props into position.

Imagine the excitement of waiting for a vaudeville troupe to take the stage or the first-run showing of *The Wizard of Oz* in all its brilliant Technicolor glory. Think about all the people who used to see shows with you: your parents and grandparents, your high school friends, your first true love. Invite them to join you in spirit.

And if the seat next to you happens to be empty, don't be surprised if you sense a spectral presence as soon as the house lights dim.

THE HOTEL PUTNAM

The Hotel Putnam is one of the most recognizable buildings in DeLand. It's also one of the city's most haunted sites.

From the outside, the Mediterranean Revival structure looks almost like it did when it opened in 1923. On the inside, however, it's fallen into disrepair. These days, the only residents who see its former glory are the ghosts who linger in its darkened corridors.

The current hotel is actually the third hotel on the site. At first, it was Henry DeLand's Grove House, a small way station nestled among acres of citrus trees. When Alfred Putnam bought it in 1885, the Putnam Inn became a favorite gathering place for winter tourists. Unfortunately, that building burned down in 1921, but no one was hurt in the fire. The economy was booming, so the hotel was rebuilt immediately—bigger, better, and this time, fireproof, with steel, concrete, and tile.

Image 40: The Hotel Putnam, once the site of stylish parties and grand soirees, is one of DeLand's most haunted locations.

You'd probably never guess it now, but the Hotel Putnam we see today was once a marvel of modern architecture. It boasted more than a hundred guest rooms, a tropical-themed dining room, a grand ballroom, and a spacious lobby with staircases on either side. It was so popular that some people reserved rooms year-round, just so they would be assured of winter accommodations. Ambassador Bert Fish lived there for a time, when he wasn't on duty in the Middle East; you'll meet him a little later.

Because it's so close to the Athens Theatre, the Putnam even became something of a secret trysting spot for actors and actresses. They could cut through the hotel's backyard and be in their rooms—or back on stage—within the span of five minutes, depending on their performance.

Over time, however, the once-grand hotel fell into ever-deepening disrepair. The elegant social lounges were converted into dive bars with cheap beer and eighties rock bands. The tasteful guest rooms became low-rent apartments, which in turn became a refuge for drug dealers, addicts, prostitutes, and tortured souls. The old hotel was a haven for danger and even death: in 1984, a young man murdered his pregnant girlfriend there, pushing her off a third-floor fire escape in a blackout haze of drugs and alcohol.

Since then, several ghost hunters and investigators have explored the old hotel. All of them report feelings of sadness emanating from its walls. The sixth floor is possibly the most haunted, possibly due to its elevation. High above New York Avenue, the upper floors boast panoramic views of old and new DeLand.

Some visitors have seen shadowy figures in the hallways. Others say they hear footsteps. Some have even heard whistling, almost as if a bellhop is returning to his post, pleased with the shiny gold piece he received for his service.

Image 41: A bellhop poses on the grounds of the Putnam House in 1885.

ON LOCATION: THE HOTEL PUTNAM

225 West New York Avenue, DeLand

The Putnam has been in varying stages of reconstruction and remodeling for years, but the day may come when you can rent a room or an apartment in the grand old hotel. If you do—or even if you simply pass by on the street—keep your eyes open for the bellhops who used to carry bags and run errands for hotel guests. Most were young, strong, and agile, and they still dart energetically around the grounds. I've sensed the presence of an adolescent spirit there, a young boy named Tommy, who looks a lot like the bellhop photographed at the Putnam House in 1885. It's possible that he would still welcome a tip from an appreciative guest.

SCHOOL SPIRITS

Ever since Henry DeLand founded Stetson University, the school and the city have been inextricably linked. The college campus is practically a city park. Its two hundred acres of green lawn are dotted with historic buildings, a vintage world's-fair fountain, and more than a few ghosts.

The school's haunted history dates back to 1884, when Henry DeLand opened DeLand Academy and built DeLand Hall, a stick-style, Second Empire building that still serves as the school's headquarters. Its gabled roof projects an air of mystery, and a tall, imposing tower rises above the front door. Today, the walls are painted ivory with blue trim—but when you see DeLand Hall after sunset, clothed in the shadows of night, it could easily be mistaken for the Addams Family mansion.

Image 42: DeLand Hall, built in 1884, is still the main administration building for Stetson University.

If walls could talk, DeLand Hall would speak volumes. This is the place, for example, where the conniving Dr. Forbes conspired to take down his mentor and benefactor, John Stetson. After Forbes left the school in disgrace, Charles Farriss filled in for him; you'll meet the old professor of Greek later in this book, and you'll find him floating around in DeLand Hall too.

Believe it or not, the oldest building on campus isn't the most haunted. For that honor, you'll have to look next door, to Elizabeth Hall. This is the landmark architectural marvel that Mr. Stetson built to honor his beautiful young wife. The structure also houses Lee Chapel, dedicated to their son Ben, who died at the age of six. Both sites are hotspots of supernatural activity.

Look the other direction, to the north, and you'll see the remains of Hulley Tower—which is a real, actual cemetery crypt, complete with dead bodies that have been entombed there for many years. And just past the old mausoleum, you'll find Chaudoin Hall, where a murdered caretaker still stands guard over the structure and the students in his care.

THE GHOST OF ELIZABETH HALL

Elizabeth Hall is a landmark building on the Stetson University campus. It's a classic Colonial Revival, built in 1892 and modeled after Independence Hall in Stetson's hometown of Philadelphia. Decorative wood lintels embellish windows on the second story. French doors open onto a third-story balcony, which features small classical columns. A four-story pavilion rises from the center, crowned by a domed cupola. It used to house a set of eleven heavy cast-iron bells, until the belfry started to crack under their weight and the chimes were moved to their own tower.

Inside Elizabeth Hall, staircases of dark polished wood rise from a central corridor, gently conducting students, faculty, and staff toward classrooms and offices on every floor. The stately old building feels like a sacred place, where most people drop their voices to a whisper.

In the early morning hours, just as the sun rises, those who pass by Elizabeth Hall often see a young woman in a rear window, gazing out from a landing between the first and second floors. Her image is clear: she wears a blouse with a high ruffled collar, and her long hair is piled loosely in a pompadour, like a Gibson girl of the early 1900s. She seems to be looking at the landmark Holler Fountain in the courtyard, which once drew crowds at the 1939 World's Fair in New York.

Image 43: John Stetson paid for the construction of Elizabeth Hall, which was named in honor of his wife.

People inside Elizabeth Hall have seen her too. Most think she's a real person at first, except for the fact that she's dressed in odd, old-fashioned clothing. Her ruffled blouse is paired with a narrow, full-length skirt, typical of the Edwardian era. She stands casually near the stairwell, with her elbow on the railing and her hand on her chin, and she smiles pleasantly at people walking by. One morning, a custodian sweeping the stairs saw her and started to admonish her. "The building's not open yet," he said. "You should probably go back to your dorm room." As he finished his sentence, she faded from view.

Some think the specter is the ghost of Elizabeth Stetson, a church musician who charmed men wherever she went. She looked young throughout her life, even after her first husband died and she was remarried to a rich Portuguese count. While Mr. Stetson left this world before he and the school's board of trustees had fully reconciled their differences, Elizabeth continued to be a generous donor to the university. It's very possible that she stops by to enjoy the elegant academic hall that was built in her honor.

Image 44: Elizabeth Shindler married John Stetson in 1884.

Others think the ghost is a former student whose name has been lost, but whose story continues to inspire. She came to Stetson at the turn of the last century, whip smart and dedicated to her studies. Sadly, she came down with a terminal illness—but rather than go home to die, she devoted her final days to learning as much as she could, while she still had time. When she was too weak to climb the stairs of Elizabeth Hall, her classmates would carry her in their arms. She would lie on a makeshift pallet of blankets and pillows in the classrooms, listening to lectures and taking part in scholarly discussions until the day she passed away.

THE CHOIRMASTER IN THE CHAPEL

The south wing of Elizabeth Hall houses Lee Chapel, a seven-hundred-seat sanctuary with stained glass windows and a massive pipe organ. Music students from around the world come to Stetson just for the opportunity to play the organ, a wade Beckerath with two thousand, five hundred pipes, which range from the size of a pencil to eighteen feet long.

It's not unusual for faculty, staff, and students to hear the organ being played at all hours, day and night, as aspiring performers take turns. Not all of the musicians who practice, however, are in physical form. More than once, passersby have wandered into the chapel, entranced by the organ's haunting chords and melodies, only to find an empty stage.

Students who choose to play the organ after hours also know they're not alone. They feel the presence of one of Stetson's most-loved music professors, Claude Almand.

CLAUDE M. ALMAND
Dean of Music School

Image 45: Claude Almand was dean of Stetson's School of Music in the 1950s.

A charismatic Cajun man from Louisiana, Dr. Almand became the dean of Stetson's School of Music in 1953. Unfortunately, he was killed in a car crash four years later.

A minor thing like death hasn't stopped him from encouraging new generations of young music students. One former undergrad remembers practicing late at night, when he hit the G7 chord with a dramatic flourish. For a brief moment, floodlights illuminated a pair of men's dress shoes at the edge of the stage. Then the lights dimmed, and the shoes disappeared. Others report that when they play the G7 chord, they see Dean Almand's face in a mirror on the organ.

G7, as it turns out, was Dean Almand's seat in the auditorium.

THE CARETAKER OF CHAUDOIN HALL

Every haunted building seems to have doors that open and close on their own, mysterious footsteps in empty hallways, and lights that turn on and off by themselves. Few people can ever explain why.

Chaudoin Hall, Girls Dormitory,
J. B. Stetson University, De Land, Fla.

Image 46: The ghost of a murdered building superintendent still safeguards Chaudoin Hall.

In Chaudoin Hall, one of Stetson's dormitories, the reason is clear.

On a bright Christmas morning in 1930, the school's building superintendent was called to Chaudoin Hall. A suspicious character had been seen breaking and entering, and P. D. Edmunds headed over to check it out.

He discovered a young farmhand, Clayton Bell, stealing from students who had gone home for Christmas. Caught red-handed, the burglar panicked and shot Edmunds dead.

Justice was "swift and fierce." The murderer was arrested the next day, and he confessed. After two days, he was indicted, arraigned, and pleaded not guilty. The court appointed an attorney, and the trial started immediately. Jury selection took fifteen minutes, the judge heard testimony, and the prosecutor offered closing arguments. The whole process, from start to finish, took all of thirteen minutes. Jurors deliberated for just six minutes, then found Bell guilty of first-degree murder. The next morning, the judge sentenced Bell to death. He was executed on January 27, 1931, "one month and one day" after the crime was committed.

While his killer no longer poses any danger, Edmunds still watches over Chaudoin Hall. Students who live there routinely report that their doorknobs turn at night, as though someone is checking the locks. When they pop their heads out into the hall to see who it might be, the corridors are empty.

REST IN PEACE

On moonlit nights, a kindly older couple walks their dog across the campus of Stetson University. The man wears a suit and bow tie; his wife favors long drop-waist dresses, and her wavy silver hair is twisted into a chignon at the nape of her neck. They're a friendly couple. They'll nod and smile from a distance, and if their paths cross with others, they'll even stop to chat for a moment.

Look away, however, and they'll disappear in the blink of an eye. To find them again, you'll have to visit the school's Hulley Memorial, where Lincoln and Eloise Hulley have been interred for almost a hundred years.

Back in her day, Eloise loved the bells that rang from the cupola of Elizabeth Hall. Morning and night, music students and teachers alike played them, pushing wood levers and pedals to ring hymns and classical music. When the cupola started cracking under the weight of the bells, the chimes had to come down—and Eloise was devastated.

Image 47: The ghosts of Lincoln and Eloise Hulley, entombed in the Hulley Memorial Tower, slip out to walk their dog at night.

Her husband, Lincoln, was president of Stetson University for thirty years. He was a remarkable speaker, and he earned enough as a speaker on the Chautauqua circuit to keep the couple financially secure. He preached on campus too. Local ministers complained that he was stealing their thunder—and their Sunday attendance. Off campus, he used his way with words to win a seat in the Florida State Senate, and he ran for governor in 1920.

Throughout his tenure at the school, from 1904 to 1934, Lincoln also wrote poetry and plays. He even spearheaded the construction of a campus theater so his work could be performed. "My plays," he bragged, "are better than Shakespeare's." The head of the theater department, Irving Stover, wasn't as enthusiastic, but he knew who signed his paycheck, so for years, hapless drama students trod the boards with Lincoln's lines on their lips.

He clearly had a flair for drama and spectacle. A lot of his work was based on ancient myths and legends, along with the Book of Revelation. He even used hospital wards and graveyard settings for dramatic effect.

When Eloise's chimes had to come down from the cupola in Elizabeth Hall, Lincoln came up with a theatrical way to keep his wife happy. He commissioned a new tower, at his own expense, one that would soar a hundred and sixteen feet toward heaven. From the Hulley Tower, the bells could ring loud and clear—and someday, the Hulleys themselves could be laid to rest beneath them, so Eloise could enjoy the bells for all eternity.

Image 48: The Hulley Tower once stood a hundred and sixteen feet tall. Today, only the base remains, housing the earthly remains of Lincoln and Eloise Hulley.

Lincoln had a heart attack and died in 1934, before the tower was even finished. He was the first to be buried in the crypt at the base of the tower, while workers completed the structure above him. When his favorite dog died, the little spaniel was tucked in beside him. Eloise lived for another twenty-five years, until she finally joined them both in 1959.

The Eloise Chimes played on for decades, but years of wind and rain and hurricanes took their toll on the red brick belltower. Over time, the structure began to crumble. School administrators worried that it would collapse in a hailstorm of falling bricks that would leave even more people dead at its foundation. A crew carefully dismantled it in 2006, being careful not to disturb the Hulleys as they worked.

Today, only the base remains. While it's a lot less impressive than it used to look, it still shields the Hulleys in their vaults. You can even see their tombs if you stand on the concrete apron at the foundation of the tower and press your nose up against the casement windows.

If you want to see the Hulleys themselves, it's almost as easy. Simply take a stroll across the Stetson campus and look for the friendly old couple walking their dog.

ON LOCATION: STETSON UNIVERSITY

421 N. Woodland Boulevard, DeLand

Two Stetson librarians coordinate walking ghost tours of the most haunted sites on campus. Kelly Larson, an archivist, works with Hunter Murphy, a learning and engagement specialist.

They've developed the tours to share spooky stories—and to reveal the truth of the school's historic past. They describe long-standing legends, with a focus on facts, evidence, and research methods. Along the way, however, they've both gained newfound respect for the ghosts they encounter. Kelly even had a personal experience with the spirit of Eloise Hulley—and now she tries to steer clear of the Hulley Memorial.

"After our first event," she said, "I went home and dreamed all night long that I was locked in a crypt and that people were staring in the windows at me." She shuddered at the memory and laughed nervously. "Now I make Hunter do that part of the tour."

THE LIVING HISTORY MUSEUM

For almost fifty years, Professor Charles Farriss taught Greek at Stetson University. He used to brag that he never missed a class. He wasn't even late.

Now that the old professor is perpetually late, having died in 1938, he's still an ever-present figure. When he's not haunting the administration building, DeLand Hall, or his old classroom next door in Elizabeth Hall, you can find him at home, a block from campus. You can even visit him there: these days, his house is a history museum.

It's called the DeLand House now, in honor of the city's founder, but Henry DeLand never actually lived here. The first settler was George Hamlin, who built a simple farmhouse and planted an orange grove. He, in turn, sold the house to John Stetson, who probably rented it to Stetson University instructors.

Image 49: The Farriss Family: Charles, Alma, and son Carl.

Charles Farriss bought the house in 1903—and that's where he would stay for almost forty years, along with his wife, Alma. In 1938, at the age of eighty-one, Charles passed away in an upstairs bedroom. After a quick trip downtown for embalming, the undertaker brought his body back to the house so his friends, colleagues, and students could say their final goodbyes.

Charles and Alma had been married on Christmas Day, 1889. They welcomed a son, Carl, in 1892, the same year they moved to DeLand. Three years later, a daughter was born, but sadly, she died in infancy.

The young Farriss family was a popular addition to the Stetson community. Both were professors. While Charles focused on the classics, Alma taught piano and domestic science. She also founded the Woman's Club of DeLand, a progressive group that promoted women's voting rights, free kindergarten, public education, and health care.

Image 50: The Farriss family home is now a history museum.

Over the years, Charles and Alma transformed the little farmhouse into an impressive Classical Revival estate. They moved the main entrance from the south side to the east side of the house, facing the Stetson campus. They added a full second story and a stately Greek Revival portico, complete with Roman columns. Charles also enjoyed making stained glass, so he crafted windows for the entryways and back parlor, as well as inlays for the fireplace and some cabinet doors.

Alma managed their home life, while Charles was a stereotypical absentminded professor. Students took his Greek and Latin classes for an easy A, because everyone knew he was too nice to give anyone an F. They could even use printed translations during tests, when they should have been translating the text on their own. When his colleagues questioned the wisdom of giving his students open access to all the answers, the trusting Dr. Farriss was appalled. "My students wouldn't cheat!" he exclaimed.

"His mind was not of the very highest order," historian Gilbert Lycan concluded, "but it was unalloyed by dross."

Image 51: Charles Farriss, professor of Greek, pictured in 1932.

Other colleagues thought of him as the most trusting man on campus, with a simple, childlike faith in God and fellow man.

During the Forbes scandal, when the president of the school was seen cavorting with one of the teachers, Charles could never believe that a school administrator would abuse his power over a subordinate. He also couldn't imagine that a man he knew and respected could ever cheat on his wife. The rest of the campus was bitterly divided by the accusations, but the cheerful Dr. Farriss carried on with his own routine, disregarding any controversy. When the school needed an interim president to fill in after Forbes left, Farriss could step in without ruffling anyone's feathers. Years later, when Lincoln Hulley died suddenly, Farris would serve as acting president a second time. By then, however, he would be seventy-seven and in poor health.

Stetson had no retirement plan, so Charles Farris kept plugging along, all through the first World War, the roaring twenties, the Depression, and the buildup to World War II. While history marched forward, Professor Farriss wandered back and forth between his house and the Stetson campus, where he spent his days thinking about ancient Greece and Rome.

He never missed a class until Friday, February 11, 1938, when he was too weak to walk to work. He languished for two months, seeing visitors at home until his doctor cut them off. In April, the board of trustees voted to award him a life salary starting in the fall, but Charles Farriss wouldn't live to collect his reward. He died just six days later.

Alma stayed in the house until 1943, when she fell down the stairs. Her son, Carl, brought her to his house in North Carolina, where he worked for the government. A week later, she had a stroke and died.

Other families came and went. Eventually, the Farriss house was converted into apartments. In 1988, a donor gave the house to the West Volusia Historical Society, and in 1990, the museum officially opened its doors.

Bill Dreggors, the founder of the historical society, used to have an office on the second floor. When he worked evenings, his wife would go along, but she liked to sit in the parlor on the main floor, reading. One night, she was almost driven to distraction by the sound of her husband clomping up and down the stairs. On the way home, she asked, "What were you doing stomping around all night?"

He looked at her incredulously. "I don't know what you're talking about," he said. "I was at my desk the whole time."

ON LOCATION: THE DELAND HOUSE MUSEUM

137 West Michigan Avenue, DeLand

When you stop by the history center, be sure to say hello to Bill Dreggors. The fourth-generation Floridian, born in DeLand, is the folk historian who dedicated his life to preserving stories of the area's earliest days. Pull up a chair, and he'll show you photos from the archives, with colorful commentary about each one.

Image 52: Bill Dreggors, DeLand's hometown historian.

People used to call him "Mr. DeLand." Yes, he knew a lot about the city, but over time he also became the living embodiment of the town's founder. He grew a long, white beard so he looked just like Henry DeLand. When he was reenacting historical events, he wore an old-fashioned black suit, a string tie, and a broad-brimmed Stetson hat. By one count, Bill created more than a hundred and twenty historical programs focused on local landmarks, along with legends and lore passed down from original settlers.

He's not the executive director of the historical society anymore. His successor, Sarah Thorncroft, has taken over his old desk in the headquarters of the DeLand House Museum. "He's still around, though," she says. "He still comes in to keep an eye on us."

Ask to sit down with Bill, and he'll have something to tell you about every street and historic structure in the city. He talks with a folksy Florida twang and his trademark dry humor. Here's how he describes an old stone fountain, for example:

"You go back up on West New York Avenue," he says, "in front of where the Catholic church is today, and you see a horse watering trough out on the street there, where the horses could stop and refresh themselves when they're coming into town or when they're getting ready to leave … and of course, humans could drink out of it too, I guess, if they wanted to."

Bill is old and he looks his age, as anyone born in 1926 would. His blue eyes still sparkle, though, and while his voice is worn with time, most of what he says is easy enough to understand. What's more, he's available, day and night, to share facts and figures about the hometown he loved.

Granted, Bill died in 2017, but his legacy lives on. In his final years, before he left to join the old pioneers, he recorded more than fifty slide shows, documentaries, and dramatic reenactments—all categorized by topic and theme. Thanks to those tapes, Bill Dreggors's electronic ghost is the easiest ghost to find in all of Volusia County.

THE WIZARD'S DEATH MASK

The death mask shows a man at peace, the hint of a smile, a forehead only gently lined. Lue Gim Gong has been dead for more than a hundred years, but we can still see his face, exactly as he looked in life.

Hours after the Chinese immigrant died, an art professor from Stetson University rushed to preserve his likeness in a plaster mold, summoned to his deathbed by DeLand's business leaders. They wanted to immortalize the man who had single-handedly saved the citrus industry—the humble gardener everyone called "the Citrus Wizard."

Gim Gong was born in China, where his mother taught him how to create sweeter fruit by gently dusting orange blossoms with pollen from other trees. He left home with his uncle at the age of twelve, eager to see the world. After a two-month journey across the Pacific, he landed in San Francisco in 1872. He found work in a shoe factory, but soon he was recruited to travel even further, to another factory in Massachusetts where workers had gone on strike.

In the Bay State, churchgoers volunteered to teach Chinese immigrants to read and speak English. The young Gim Gong was paired with Frances "Fannie" Burlingame, forty-four. It couldn't have been a better match. She was a mathematician, botanist, and cousin to the former US ambassador to China. She became a second mother to the young man and invited him to live in her house. She had a huge garden and a greenhouse full of exotic plants, and Gim Gong felt truly at home.

Image 53: Lue Gim Gong single-handedly saved Florida's citrus industry by creating oranges that could survive cold snaps.

Fannie was heartsick when Gim Gong contracted tuberculosis in the mid-1880s. He couldn't stay in Massachusetts, where the cold, damp winters would only make him sicker. He traveled back to China, where the weather was better, and his parents welcomed him with open arms.

Within days, they started arranging a wedding for him. Gim Gong objected. He had converted to Christianity, for one thing, and he didn't want a Buddhist bride. More importantly, he was sick, and he didn't want to burden a young wife with a husband who might die at any minute. His parents arranged the marriage anyway. In 1886, on the night before the wedding, Gim Gong ran away and boarded a ship for San Francisco. His parents disowned him, but Fannie sent him money for a ticket to DeLand, where she had a winter home.

She had to lie to immigration authorities to get him back, because the Chinese Exclusion Act of 1882 was already in effect. Fannie subverted the ban by forging documents and listing him as a merchant.

Gim Gong settled in DeLand, where Fannie and her sister owned a citrus grove. There, surrounded by orange and grapefruit trees as far as the eye could see, he would make Florida history.

Over the years, Gim Gong created several new varieties of fruit, including the sweet Valencia orange, designed to resist the cold and frost that had decimated the orange harvest every few years. It saved the citrus industry. The American Pomological Society awarded him a Silver Wilder Medal in 1911, and everyone started calling him the Citrus Wizard.

Gim Gong also developed grapefruits, apples, peaches, and tomatoes that growers—and customers—loved. His accomplishments were even featured at the 1933 Chicago World's Fair.

He was a brilliant horticulturist but a terrible businessman. He gave away free samples of his fruit and cuttings from his plants, much to his own detriment. He struck bad deals with nurseries, who agreed to pay him for the trees they sold—and then sold seedlings, instead. He was cheated by distributors, who refused to pay for materials they ordered and royalties he was entitled to. He floundered in debt and came dangerously close to losing his property, until friends, neighbors, and fellow orange growers rushed to his aid. After his death, they found a trunk filled with checks he didn't know how to deposit or cash.

He was lonely too. Fannie Burlingame died in 1903. She didn't have a will, but Fannie's sisters agreed to give Gim Gong her property in DeLand, along with ten thousand dollars from her estate. At one point, Gim Gong proposed to LaGette Hagstrom, who had been Burlingame's maid and companion. She declined, and Gim Gong retreated to his hundred and fifteen acres. After that, some say he only ventured off his land a handful of times. He lived alone, with only animals to keep him company: two horses, Fanny and Baby, and a rooster named March that he had rescued from a hawk attack. And while he grew too old and frail to work, he always welcomed visitors, and he often prayed with them in the gazebo in his yard.

Lue Gim Gong died on June 3, 1925, and was buried in DeLand's Oakdale Cemetery. Hundreds of people came to his funeral. Obituaries around the world praised his accomplishments. Over time, however, his name faded from memory, and his accomplishments were nearly forgotten.

ON LOCATION: THE LUE GIM GONG MEMORIAL GARDEN

West Volusia Historical Society, 137 West Michigan Avenue, DeLand

Today you can sit with the life-sized bust of Lue Gim Gong in his memorial garden, where his death mask has been transformed into a striking bronze bust. It's the centerpiece of the Lue Gim Gong Memorial Garden at the West Volusia Historical Society. Just look for his gazebo surrounded by orange trees.

The tribute was a long time coming. After he died in 1925, DeLand's leaders displayed the death mask to raise funds for a sculpture in his memory. Before the project could get underway, two hurricanes hit Florida, land values plummeted, the banks crashed, and America sank into the Great Depression.

Decades later, however, the tribute was revived, and the monument was finally dedicated in 1999. Today, the Lue Gim Gong Memorial Garden highlights the grounds of the DeLand House Museum.

When you visit, take a seat on one of the built-in benches and spend a few minutes enjoying his company. If you happen to spot a ripe Valencia in the trees nearby, go ahead and enjoy the orange too. Gim Gong won't mind.

JUSTICE IS SERVED

On your way to the Haunted Antique Shop, you'll probably drive past the historic Volusia County Courthouse. Its massive copper dome, green with the patina of age, rises high above the downtown business district. The old clocktower still chimes the hours, marking each moment as it ticks away and recording every passing day as it becomes another page in the annals of history.

Image 54: Volusia County's historic courthouse opened in 1929.

These days, trials and hearings take place in a new, modern courthouse a few blocks away. That leaves the old courthouse available for Volusia County's ghosts to carry on with the legal issues they cared about, back when the courthouse was new.

It's where you'll find haunting echoes of political corruption and legal coercion—but not among the defendants who used to find themselves on trial here. In Volusia County's early days, some of the shadiest characters in court were the lawyers and judges who walked these halls.

You can trace their footsteps back to the first class of the first law school in Florida, over at Stetson University. That's where the improbably named Bert Fish, a poor boy who wanted to get rich, met his future law partner—a professor named Cary Landis. It's also where the seeds were planted for a political ploy that had global ramifications. We'll get to that in a bit.

Bert Fish came with his parents to DeLand when he was only five. Throughout his youth, he was small for his age, and he looked awkward and self-conscious in all his school photos. His eyes were dark and beady, and he had a receding chin, big ears, and wild red hair that wouldn't lay flat until he started going bald years later.

Image 55: Bert Fish was a shrewd lawyer who made millions at a time when most people were desperately poor.

As a child, he helped his parents in their Fish market, which sadly wasn't really a fish market but an eponymously named general store. To their credit, at least they had a big fish painted above the door. After his father died, young Bert helped support the family any way he could: working in other shops, sorting mail, and eventually teaching. Along the way, he started making political connections, clerking in the state senate during the late 1890s. Back in Volusia County, he served as superintendent of schools.

And then, when Stetson University started its law program, he was one of the first legal scholars to enroll. When Bert Fish graduated, he and his law professor Cary Landis opened a practice on Indiana Avenue, right next to the courthouse.

From that point on, Bert Fish was unstoppable in his drive for political power and financial success. The new law partners built an impressive Romanesque-style office building, which grew to a two-story Federal structure in 1925. Fish and Landis did stints as prosecutors and judges. Along the way, they also organized a cozy political coalition that controlled most of the elections in the county—the Democrat "Courthouse Ring."

I. A. STEWART.
(Stewart & Bly.)

Image 56: Isaac Stewart was a hot-headed attorney who railed against his political enemies.

Fish and Landis weren't the only lawyers in town. Right across the street, their legal adversaries had their own law practice, led by Arthur Hamlin, DeLand's first attorney, and Isaac Stewart, a rabble-rousing, dirt-digging firebrand. Before long, they were political opponents too. Hamlin and Stewart formed an opposition group to counter the Courthouse Ring—the inventively monikered "Anti-Ring."

Isaac Stewart was a hothead. He would often stand in the street, shouting and shaking his fist in Bert Fish's direction. He even went so far as to put a sound system on the roof of his building, so he could blast city and county officials at full volume.

Their conflict was partly a class struggle. Most of Isaac's clients were ordinary people of modest means, while Fish and Landis represented big business. They catered to banks, municipal governments, public utilities, and railroads.

Bert Fish paid close attention to his clients' legal affairs, and he used his insider status to invest in real estate deals with incredible returns. By 1923, his real estate portfolio alone was worth five hundred thousand dollars. His holdings included six commercial buildings, two hotels, the entire south shore of a nearby lake, and several thousand acres of citrus groves.

Bert Fish also invested in like-minded politicians. He doled out patronage like party favors, ensuring that his friends and allies would win every local election, by hook or by crook. When Fish himself ran for state senate in 1916, arch-rival Isaac Stewart snarled that Fish was nothing more than a corrupt political boss who exercised "monstrous power... with all the money he wanted."

Bert Fish loved the high life. At a time when most people were still relegated to travel by horses and wagons, or even mule carts, he raced luxury cars up and down DeLand's dusty streets. He started with a Cadillac Roadster, then upgraded to an even more luxurious Stearns touring car.

He earned enough money to retire at the age of fifty-two. He sold his share of the law firm and started traveling around the Mediterranean. His political interest didn't fade, though. When Franklin Delano Roosevelt ran for president, Fish donated five thousand dollars to his campaign. That was enough to buy himself an ambassador's post in Egypt. Ultimately, Fish served as a foreign diplomat for seven years in Egypt and one year in Portugal.

Image 57: Ambassador Bert Fish enjoys a garden lunch with Egypt's Prince Mohamed Ali Pasha in 1936.

But this is where we get to a plot twist. Maybe it was his background in backroom politics, glad-handing people in power, and engaging in questionable dirty deals, but Bert Fish was an *amazing* ambassador. He was one of the first citizen diplomats, and he took to international relations like a... well, a fish to water. He loved the Egyptian people, for one thing, and he helped them liberate themselves from British and French rule. Because he introduced himself as a simple citrus farmer from Florida, the Egyptians called him the "Orange King." And as World War II began, Bert Fish was in position to secure the Suez Canal, keep oil reserves away from Hitler and Mussolini, and limit our enemies' access to other war resources in Portugal. World War II was touch-and-go until the very end. Without Bert Fish's influence, the Allies could have lost the war.

Bert Fish died before he knew that victory was assured. Official reports said he had a heart attack. Some rumors said he was murdered, but the war took precedence over a full investigation. Back in DeLand, an impressive array of diplomats, world leaders, and heads of state came to his funeral.

So not only did Bert Fish save the free world, but after his death, he saved countless lives in his hometown. He had never married or had a family, so he left his entire fortune, worth millions of dollars, to the people of Volusia County. His money built two hospitals, one each in DeLand and New Smyrna Beach, along with a new wing for the Sanford Hospital. To this day, the money he left in trust still earns interest, and it still pays for health care all over Central Florida.

Some people believe that as long as your name is remembered, you'll never truly die. That's why the pharaohs built their pyramids—as timeless monuments to help assure their immortality.

Bert Fish left his name on his buildings in DeLand, of course. He also left a legacy of health and hope through the hospitals he founded. And if that wasn't enough, he left an impressive array of Egyptian treasures to be enshrined in the halls of his alma mater, Stetson University. His collection included a library of rare books dating back to Napoleon's explorations. Inside, he mounted his own bookplates, inscribed in hieroglyphics.

Here's a translation. Read it in your spookiest voice.

[In front of the scribe] That which is in the library
of the Judge of the High Court Bert son of Fish born of
the Mistress of the house Sarah, daughter of Lee. He is
Envoy to the Majesty of the King of Upper and Lower Egypt
Faruk, living forever.

ON LOCATION: THE HISTORIC VOLUSIA COUNTY COURTHOUSE

125 West New York Avenue, DeLand

Walk up the steps and through the columns that mark the entrances, and you'll feel as though you're truly walking into a twentieth-century temple of justice. The courthouse is a neoclassical building with two main entrances, a feature that architects call a double façade. The south entrance faces New York Avenue. The north entrance faces Indiana Avenue. Both are marked by tall Corinthian columns. Inside, you'll find marble staircases, oil paintings that highlight great moments in Florida history, and stained-glass windows that filter light through the overhead dome. Whether you're Pro-Ring or Anti-Ring, you'll probably agree that the courthouse itself is a monument to the rule of law.

THE HANGED MAN

In the game of chess, the rules are black and white. Pawns hope for promotion, knights fight for victory, and rooks stand stalwart against intrusion. Armies march across a field of precise angles, opponents clash in silent battles, and wars are fought without a drop of blood. It's an idealized battleground, and in DeLand, there's an entire plaza dedicated to the game: Chess Park.

Image 58: Crowds gathered in DeLand on the day Charlie Brown was hanged for murder.

Ironically, Chess Park is strategically positioned next to the old courthouse—where legal conflicts weren't always so defined.

Chess Park is a quiet retreat from the modern world with a life-size chessboard, chess tables made of concrete, and chess-shaped sculptures on pillars and walls. It's open from sunrise to sunset—but when the sun slides below the western horizon, new players come into the match. As the moon rises, DeLand's ghosts and spirits step out of the courthouse shadows, still pondering their final move.

Stand quietly, and you'll see the ghost of Charles Browne Perelli sitting at a table by the wall, his neck still caught in a hangman's noose. Look carefully, and you'll also see his attorney, Rose Falls Bres, who fought to save his life.

"Charlie Brown," as the locals called him, was tried here, sentenced here, and executed in a jail yard across the street. His earthly life came to an end on April 28, 1927. As the last man hanged in Florida, his case lives on in legend.

Brown, twenty-nine, was convicted of murdering a cab driver named Howard "Red" Usher. Brown didn't act alone: he'd been accompanied by his wife, Clara, and an accomplice named George Burns. The three of them had hired Usher to drive them from the Daytona Beach train station to Port Orange. Once they were in the cab, they robbed him, shot him three times, and left him for dead by the side of the road. Usher managed to flag down a passing motorist, and he lived long enough to describe his killers. Police found the trio of miscreants waiting for a train in Bunnell.

Brown's wife testified against him, and she was acquitted. Accomplice George Burns was sentenced to life in prison. "The damn stool pigeon squealed," Brown said later. Brown, considered to be the ringleader, was sentenced to death.

His first conviction was overturned on appeal, but then he was convicted again. He was headed for the electric chair when, at the last minute, the governor halted his execution. That's when attorney Rose Falls Bres made a final desperate appeal to the state supreme court—a last-ditch effort to save his life by insisting upon the letter of the law. Electrocution was the new law of the land, but she argued that Brown had been sentenced to death by hanging, and that was the penalty he should receive.

Bres didn't get the dismissal she wanted. Prosecutors were ready with a checkmate. Within days, a circuit judge resentenced Brown to hang, the governor signed a new death warrant, and the sheriff brought Charlie Brown back to the Volusia County Jail, where a pinewood scaffold had been hastily constructed.

On the morning of the hanging, crowds gathered bright and early. More than two thousand spectators came to watch. Not only did they revile Charlie Brown, but they knew it was the last public execution they would ever see. It was practically a holiday. Shops and offices closed, and citrus farmers came in from their orange groves. Schools were dismissed so children could attend. Onlookers crowded the street, and some stood on rooftops to get a better view.

CHARLIE BROWN

Image 59: Charlie Brown was the last man hanged in the state of Florida.

The sheriff met Brown in his cell and tied his hands behind his back. Then he and three deputies led the convict up the thirteen steps to the gallows, put a black hood over his head, and slipped a noose around his neck. A presbyterian minister prayed.

The sheriff asked, "Charlie Brown, are you ready?"

Brown didn't answer. Earlier, he had already uttered his last words. "Great sins have been forgiven," he said.

Image 60: Attorney Rose Falls Bres did her best to save Charlie Brown from the hangman's noose.

The trap door sprang open at 10:06 a.m., and Brown plummeted through the gaping void. The rope jerked, then began to swing back and forth, hitting the opening on either side over and over again. Brown's neck was broken, but he still had a pulse, and his body twitched reflexively. For twenty-four minutes, Brown swayed at the end of the rope, while the crowd watched in horrified silence. At 10:30, a doctor finally pronounced him dead.

The children who watched the execution were traumatized. Decades later, one of them said that afterward, he wouldn't even pick up a pencil off the street, for fear that he'd be accused of theft and hanged.

Rose Falls Bres was both traumatized and disgusted. She later described the execution in her ongoing attempts to eradicate the death penalty.

"It was a barbaric picnic party," she wrote. "In this execution there was the real hundred percent thrill of witnessing the twitching for nearly thirty minutes of a young man, hung by the neck by 'due process of law.'"

Brown was buried in a pauper's grave near the county poor farm, about a mile from downtown DeLand.

Years earlier, Ben Franklin had mused on the parallels between the game of life and the game of chess.

"Life is a kind of chess," he wrote, *"in which we have often points to gain, and competitors or adversaries to contend with, and in which there is a vast variety of good and ill events."*

ON LOCATION: CHESS PARK

116 Indiana Avenue, DeLand

Chess Park is open from sunrise to sunset. It's surprisingly peaceful: street noise is blocked by the old courthouse on one side and Bert Fish's law office on the other. If you play chess, you can bring your own pieces or borrow a set from the newspaper office across the street. You can also rent life-size chess pieces there, though you'll probably have to arrange that in advance.

Chess Park might also be the most picturesque park in town, so bring your camera. By day, it's an oasis where you can enjoy a takeout lunch or visit with friends. At night, it's lit with strings of patio lights, and visitors pass through as they walk to bars, restaurants, and a nearby farmer's market.

If you're lucky, you might catch an orb or two.

YOUR HOSTS, THE BARNHILL GHOSTS

Edwin and Jeanette Barnhill had big dreams when they built the DeLand Hotel on Woodland Boulevard. They planned a budget-friendly retreat for middle-class travelers, like themselves. The building looked like a Mediterranean resort, and winter tourists were drawn to stucco walls and arched façades. While the forty guest rooms were small, they were cheap, and they were comfortable. The hotel's location meant guests could walk up and down main street, shopping and stopping at cafés and restaurants along the way. On sunny days, the Barnhills' guests could even pile into an open-air bus—which was actually two Model Ts welded together—and head off on a whirlwind day trip to Daytona Beach.

DELAND HOTEL, DELAND, FLA.

Image 61: From the outside, the hotel on South Woodland Avenue still looks like it did when it was built in 1924.

The Barnhills' future should have been as sunny and bright as the Florida sky. Sadly, the life they hoped to build together would never come to be. Just four years after they built the hotel, Jeanette Barnhill died. A year later, Edwin was declared insane.

Some say it was Jeanette's ghost that drove him mad. Edwin and Jeanette fought while they were both alive, and they continued to spar even after Jeanette's death. She hounded him about his drinking, turning lights off to save money, and pinching pennies wherever possible. Later, hotel guests reported that Edwin frequently yelled at his wife's ghost, demanding that she stop looking over his shoulder while he did the books.

Mrs. E. D. Barnhill, long familiar with hotel management, whose dreams are largely embodied in the new DeLand Hotel.

E. D. Barnhill, proprietor of DeLand's newest hotel, which was formally opened to the public on Feb. 9.

Image 62: Jeanette and Edwin Barnhill still haunt their old hotel on DeLand's main street.

Other owners stepped in. The hotel was popular during the 1930s and 1940s, but after that, it slowly spiraled into a deep decline. It became a refuge for troubled guests, many of whom were mired in alcohol, drugs, and prostitution. It wasn't a tourist destination anymore; beds were rented by the month, week, even the hour. A prostitute was strangled on the premises. At one point during the hotel's long decline, a troubled guest refused to leave his room. When the police came, he told them that an old woman in 1920s clothing had told him not to leave.

The hotel eventually closed in 1985 and stood abandoned for years. In 1997, investors bought the property. They consolidated the forty small rooms into eight suites and reopened it as boutique hotel in 1999.

When they were alive, the Barnhills lived in a small room on the second floor. Some say they never left. Even now, guests and employees have reported seeing the Barnhills on the premises. While Jeanette seems to haunt the second floor near her old room, Edwin's ghost lingers in the basement.

Others have encountered a young girl looking for her mother. She says her name is Sara Elizabeth, and she tugs on their sleeves. Some glimpse the

troubled prostitute who was strangled there, along with other shadowy figures in doorways. They hear footsteps and whistling in empty rooms and
corridors. Dishes fly off shelves in the hotel kitchen. Sometimes, a mysterious blue light floats through an upstairs hallway.

The Barnhills' hotel is no longer a troubled property. Even so, it's still
just as haunted as ever. Maybe that's because Edwin and Jeanette, freed
from their financial burdens, can finally enjoy the beautiful hotel they built.

ON LOCATION: THE HAUNTED HOTEL

215 South Woodland Boulevard, DeLand

Image 63: The windows of the Barnhill hotel now feature painted
vignettes of former guests.

During the 1990s renovation, some of the hotel's windows had to be
blocked in. Rather than leave them an eyesore, though, the owners hired
Courtney Canova and Doug Harris to paint vignettes in each space. The
life-size images look like guests—or ghosts—in period clothing from the
hotel's heydays of the 1930s and '40s.

THE HAUNTED MANSION

The old Dutton House on DeLand's New York Avenue looks like something out of a horror movie: a crumbling mansion locked behind a chain-link fence. Some siding is missing, some trim has fallen, and ornamental details have been stripped away—but the house still beckons, like an old woman with a snaggle-toothed smile, desperately trying to remind us that she once was young and beautiful. Diamond-paned windows reflect light from the sun and shadows from the moon, casting the illusion of life within its vacant walls.

Image 64: The John Dutton house in DeLand was a mansion turned mortuary. This photo shows some of the Dutton children with their nurse in 1911, back when the house was new.

Maybe that's because there is life inside—along with death. Both are remnants from the house's long and haunted history. First it was a mansion, and then it was a mortuary.

Seven children grew up here, back when the house was new. They chased up and down its grand staircase and sang and danced on a custom stage their father built. On hot summer nights, they slept on the verandas, side by side, where they could dream beneath a star-filled sky.

The stately old home might be a shell of its former self, but the walls still safeguard its most distinctive features, including mirrored fireplaces and mahogany trim. Surprisingly, considering its age, no one ever remodeled or redecorated the interior in any way that would destroy its historical significance. Ornate ceiling medallions mark the spots where glittering chandeliers used to cast their shimmering light. A grand piano still graces a music room, where windows span the walls from floor to ceiling. Ghostly hands drift across its dusty keys, while distant strains of Bach and Beethoven linger in the air.

When it was new, in 1911, the neoclassical manor was one of DeLand's most elegant homes. It was also the most ornate. There were bastions of tall Corinthian columns on two sides of the house, holding tiered verandas overlooking the landscaped yard. The exterior walls were crowned with a roof of ceramic tile. The eaves were adorned with scrolling brackets and tooth-shaped dentils, like an ornamental picture frame.

John Wesley Dutton, a wealthy merchant, paid $25,000 for its construction. The Georgia native had made his fortune in the lumber trade. His business controlled much of the turpentine harvest at the turn of the century, when the pine extract was one of Central Florida's main industries. With 11,000 square feet of living space, the massive three-story structure had plenty of room for John, his wife Lilla, and their brood of boys and girls.

The children grew up, and John and Lilla grew old. After John died in the 1920s, Lilla sold the house to Jesse and Mercedes Stith. Over the years, the Stiths had thousands of overnight guests—but they were all quiet and unobtrusive, because they were dead. The Stiths were morticians, and they ran a funeral parlor in the house through most of the 1940s.

When the Stiths joined their clientele in the cemetery, the house was converted into apartments. Over time, the building began to fall into ruin. Repairs were delayed, and routine maintenance was deferred. Eventually, it was condemned and slated for demolition, until a publishing executive from Fort Lauderdale snapped it up in a last-minute rescue bid. He had health problems, so preservationists stepped in. They were able to stabilize the roof and exterior walls while they search for funds to renovate the interior.

It stands now in limbo, a tattered ghost, beckoning us to bring it back to life.

ON LOCATION: THE DUTTON HOUSE

332 West New York Avenue, DeLand

Most of us can only imagine living in a mansion as elegant as the Dutton House. It's even harder to imagine when a house is in disrepair. Walk by the old house, however, and you'll soon realize that the long-standing estate is more than a local landmark. It's a monument to a different time.

While it's still being renovated, the house isn't safe for wanderers, so don't trespass. You're free to drive past or look from the sidewalk. If you want to see inside, you'll find plenty of photos online.

NIGHT SHIFT

Dr. Senator Ruben Coleman knew the deck was stacked against him. He was a skilled physician, with degrees in medicine and pharmacology. He was passionate about the healing arts and determined to build a practice that would move small-town medical care into the modern era.

But Dr. Coleman was black, and in 1918, that meant the whole country would have to make major strides before he could make the most of his skills. Eventually, Dr. Coleman would make progress, but only when the unequal treatment of DeLand's white and black patients was too great for anyone to ignore.

Today, DeLand's Memorial Hospital and Veterans Museum stands as a monument, both to the injustices of the past and the courage of those who fought for change. More than a century has passed since it housed patients, but even now, the shadowy figures of former doctors and nurses still haunt the grounds. Some people swear they've seen ghostly faces peering through the windows. Others say spirits linger in the gardens and gazebo on the lawn.

Image 65: Dr. S. R. Coleman was DeLand's first black physician.

Back in 1918, Dr. Coleman was the city's first black physician. Before he opened a practice in his home on Howry Avenue, most black people rarely received professional care. His private clinic was a start, but he could only work under the supervision of a white doctor, and he could only treat people of color.

What's more, he couldn't arrange intensive care for his sickest patients. They weren't allowed in the emergency facility that opened during the 1918 Spanish flu epidemic or into the DeLand Memorial Hospital that opened in 1921. Both were for whites only. Instead, he sent his sickest patients to recuperate at the home of his nurse, a midwife named Amanda Walker Worthy.

DeLand's new hospital was an imposing three-story structure on Stone Street, not far from Dr. Coleman's house. It stood at the top of a hill, overlooking a wide, expansive lawn. Even now, the Italian Renaissance structure looks more like a hotel than a hospital.

Black leaders like James Wright and his brother, Tony Wright, wanted better health care for their community too. They convinced Dr. Lancaster Starke, a black obstetrician, to move to DeLand, where he worked alongside black midwives like Hattie Hough and Carrie Smokes. James rented office space to Dr. Samuel Poole, a black dentist, and Dr. Starke.

The Wright brothers also raised funds for a satellite structure that would be affiliated with the new hospital. They were successful in their mission. In 1926, when the Elizabeth Roe Burgess Pavilion opened behind the hospital, black patients finally had access to hospital care. But at the same time, the differences between the pavilion and the big hospital highlighted the inequality of care.

While the hospital looked like a resort, the pavilion looked like a storage building. The hospital had spacious suites for thirty patients, a maternity ward, and an operating room. The pavilion was little more than an open space with six beds. When black patients needed access to medical equipment, technicians reluctantly wheeled it across the parking lot. And when black patients needed surgery, white doctors like Charles Tribble secretly wheeled them across the parking lot, into the hospital under cover of darkness. Sometimes they waited until after midnight to ensure that no one would see them and put a stop to their work.

Those are the shadows we see now, echoes of a past so painful that its memory remains.

As time passed, doctors, nurses, and community leaders began to fight back against discrimination. They openly decried the disparity between the two facilities, as well as the senseless regulations that kept so many patients from critical care. In 1935, the medical staff demanded a policy change, and the restrictions were dropped. Most black patients were still treated in the pavilion, however, until the hospital was outdated and closed.

Miss Amanda, the midwife, died in 1932, and Dr. Coleman worked until he died in 1945. They had seen monumental changes over the course of their careers. In 1952, the Bert Fish Memorial Hospital opened; while it had separate entrances, caregivers treated everyone—black and white alike. Segregation officially ended with the Civil Rights Act of 1964.

ON LOCATION: MEMORIAL HOSPITAL AND PAVILION

230 North Stone Street, DeLand

In the early 1990s, the Burgess Pavilion, destroyed by termites, was demolished during the restoration of the DeLand Memorial Hospital. It was rebuilt and reopened as a museum in 1993, focusing on the history and culture of black people in DeLand.

One of those exhibits features DeLand's first black dentist, Dr. Samuel William Poole. His equipment is on display, and you can even see the dental chair he used in his office in the Wright Building. For a while after he retired, he kept it in his dining room, and he sat in it for a few minutes every day. His widow donated it to the museum after he died. Look closely, and you still might see him there.

CASSADAGA, THE PSYCHIC CAPITOL OF THE WORLD

Not far from our shop, you'll find an entire village dedicated to the Spirit World. The little settlement of Cassadaga is only six miles away, on the shores of Lake Colby, just north of Spirit Pond. That's where members of the Southern Cassadaga Spiritualist Camp have been communing with ghosts and spirits since 1894.

The hamlet hasn't changed much since its founder, George P. Colby, invited fellow travelers to follow him to Florida.

Colby was a medium who offered séances around the country after the Civil War. In a nation traumatized by the bloodiest battle in its history, his services were in high demand. More than seven-hundred-and-fifty-thousand soldiers had been killed in the war between North and South. Their grieving widows, mothers, and children were desperate for assurance that those men were still with them in spirit. Mediums like Colby, who could serve as a link between the living and the dead, were literally a lifeline for families that had been divided by politics, devastated by war, and destroyed by grief.

Image 66: The Cassadaga Spiritualist Camp, just five miles from DeLand, is a national center for Spiritualist mediums and healers.

Colby had been born to Baptist parents in Pike, New York. Later, the family moved to Minnesota. At the age of twelve, he was baptized in a freezing lake. The physical shock literally took his breath away. It seems to have jump-started his psychic abilities too. After his icy baptism, Colby began to exhibit healing powers and clairvoyant abilities. His Baptist parents tried to physically beat him into submission, but Colby refused to deny his gifts. He left the Baptist church and embraced Spiritualism.

Spiritualists take it as an article of faith that souls live on after physical death, and that personal identities remain intact. They believe in afterlife communication, especially when it's facilitated by trained mediums.

Image 67: George Colby, the founder
of Cassadaga, was called "The Seer
of Spiritualism."

As a young man, Colby often attended Spiritualist meetings at Lily Dale, a campground near the town of Cassadaga, New York. The word *Cassadaga* is actually derived from the Seneca Indians; it means "rocks beneath the water."

Before long, Colby became known as the "Seer of Spiritualism." In 1875, at a séance in Ohio, Colby started channeling the spirit of an American Indian who introduced himself as "Seneca." He claimed to be Colby's spirit guide—and he said that one day, Colby would travel to Florida and establish the greatest Spiritualist camp the world had ever seen.

Colby began a long, wandering journey to Florida, making friends with other mediums along the way. Seneca guided him step by step, showing him visions of high pine hills and silvery lakes. To get to Central Florida, Colby traveled to Jacksonville by rail, then by steamboat to Blue Springs, just south of DeLand. Then he traveled by mule wagon, along a rutted path to the east. It was slow going, through wilderness thick with trees and vines.

Image 68: George Colby, third from the left, and other members of the Cassadaga Camp in the early 1900s.

When he finally arrived at the spot where Florida's Cassadaga now stands, he recognized it immediately. The lakeshore, surrounded by hills and trees, matched the vision Seneca had been showing him all along.

Today, Cassadaga still looks like it did in Colby's time. Though Colby originally started with thirty-five acres of land, the camp quickly grew to its current size of fifty-seven acres, and the winter retreat soon became a permanent settlement with about fifty homes.

The Cassadaga Hotel is probably the first building you'll notice when you drive into the camp. It's not the original hotel, which was destroyed by fire in 1926. It's also not officially part of the Spiritualist organization, which lost ownership during the Great Depression. Even so, it's worth a visit.

The hotel is filled with vintage furnishings, including two antique pianos in the bar. Have a drink or sit down for dinner in the hotel restaurant. Hotel guests can also enjoy psychic readings, séances, and personal encounters with friendly spirits. The hotel's resident ghost, Arthur, is an

NEIGHBORHOOD HAUNTS   137

Irishman who occasionally drags a chair to the end of the hall to look out the window. Guests see him there and often report the lingering scent of his gin and cigars.

When you visit Cassadaga, you'll also find a welcome center, a healing center, and a camp bookstore, as well as the Colby Memorial Temple. You can attend Spiritualist church services, healing sessions, classes, and workshops. You can even enjoy a park with a fairy trail, designed to enhance your connection to the Spirit World.

Those who live and work in Cassadaga say it's at the heart of a spiritual vortex, where energy flows freely, and the veil between this world and the next is thin.

Many residents offer readings and healings from their homes. While the structures are privately owned, the land itself belongs to the Spiritualist organization. Other psychic readers have set up camp on their own land, adjacent to the Spiritualists' property, and they offer services like tarot, astrology, and palmistry.

Cassadaga was added to the National Register of Historic Places in 1991.

ON LOCATION: THE CASSADAGA FAIRY TRAIL

1200 Chauncey Street, Cassadaga, Florida

When it was founded, some local pastors and preachers said Spiritualists were devil worshippers who conducted occult rituals and witches who practiced pagan rites.

Some of those rumors have persisted to the present day. Many people, for example, go out of their way to see the Devil's Chair in the Cassadaga Cemetery, which is actually located in nearby Lake Helen. They've heard that whoever sits in the chair will hear voices or see demonic shadows. Those who live nearby, however, point out that the chair is really just a bench, built by a man who lost his wife and needed a place to sit when he visited her grave. You can find similar benches in just about every cemetery in America.

If you're looking for a truly mystical experience, visit the Cassadaga Fairy Trail. It's in Horseshoe Park, just up the hill from the Colby Memorial Temple.

When you walk through the white pillars at the entrance of the trail, you'll step into the realm of nature spirits: pixies, gnomes, and sprites. As you stroll along the path, you'll encounter a range of art installations with whimsical details, and you'll be awed by the natural beauty that has inspired Spiritualists since George Colby settled here.

Many visitors leave small offerings to enhance the trail, like the flowered leis and sparkling beads that hang from tree limbs. Diminutive fairy houses are scattered along the walkway, and you can stop for two photo opportunities: a large green chair with fairy wings near the entrance and a free-standing fairy wings near the back.

The trail is open from dawn to dusk.

CHAPTER 5
GHOSTLY ENCOUNTERS

I remember the first spirit reading I ever did. My friend Denise wanted to know if I could tell her anything about her brother, who had died a few years earlier.

I shuffled my tarot deck and laid out the cards, face down in a ten-card Celtic Cross spread, just as I would for a living person. But as soon as I turned all the cards face up for the reading, I "heard" a voice.

It wasn't an audible voice, carried on a cold breeze or heralded with a clap of thunder. It was simply a seemingly random thought that popped into my head, complete and comprehensive, delivered in a flash. It didn't come from me. It was a message that came from the Spirit World.

"Tell her she needs to paint her house."

I was dumbfounded. Weren't messages from the Spirit World supposed to be monumental? I was expecting something more heartfelt—a call of love and longing, I guess. Since when did ghosts talk about home maintenance?

I couldn't judge whether the message sounded legitimate. I had never met Denise's brother, and I didn't know anything about him.

I paused, and I heard it again, more insistent this time. "Tell her she needs to paint her house."

Image 69: A young girl was photographed with four ghostly family members in 1905.

I took a deep breath and repeated the message. "This is going to sound really silly," I warned, "but he wants you to paint your house."

And with that, my otherwise calm, cool, and collected friend fell apart. She started crying—weeping, even.

Oh, no, I thought as I handed her a box of tissues. I feared the worst. Now she'll think I'm a fraud. She wanted me to reach out to her brother, and all I could come up with is a ridiculous passing thought that makes no sense. I'd be upset too if I were in her position.

And then she dried her eyes, wiped her nose, and said, "He's right."

I looked at her, puzzled.

"He's right. I do need to paint my house." Okay, then.

"My brother was an interior decorator," she explained, "but he died shortly after my husband and I bought our first house. One of the last things he did was decorate for us. He helped us pick out the furniture, and he chose all the colors, and he painted the walls himself. But that was ten years ago. Since then, we've had two boys, and they've colored on the walls, and they've chipped the walls with their toys, and they've left fingerprints that I can't clean off anymore because I've scrubbed them so much the paint has come off too. I know it's a mess, but I didn't want to change anything my brother did because it was the last thing he did for us."

Then she laughed. "I knew he'd be mad if he could see it," she said. "I guess I don't have an excuse for putting it off any longer."

As it turned out, my first spirit reading was actually typical of every spirit reading I've done since then. I don't deliver surprising revelations. The spirits simply come with confirmations of their continued interaction in our lives.

THE CRABBY GHOST

People's personalities don't change when they die. A few years ago, I was touring Villa Finale, a mansion in San Antonio, Texas, that had been converted into a museum. It had been the home of Walter Nold Mathis, an investor and art collector, before he died in 2005.

As we passed through the kitchen, the tour guide pointed out a wooden box with cabinet doors and asked if any of us could guess what it was.

I couldn't see anyone, but I heard a man next to me. There was no one there, but this invisible presence sounded irritated and annoyed. "It's a TV," he said, with a deep, dramatic sigh, as if he had heard the question a thousand times. Perhaps he had. I think the former owner had joined us for the tour.

Without missing a beat, I parroted his response. "It's a TV!" The tour guide looked at me, dumbfounded. "In all the time I've worked here," she said, "no one has ever guessed."

Little did she know that I never would have guessed the answer by myself, either. It took an exasperated ghost to give me the answer.

PAINLESS PASSINGS

When people die in an accident or disasters, survivors are distraught—not only by the loss, but also by fears that their loved ones suffered in their final moments. In the few cases I've experienced during readings, however, spirits have reassured us that their transition was physically painless. In one case, I read for a woman whose young son had died of smoke inhalation in a house fire. During the reading, he relayed that he had simply drifted off and that the whole thing felt like a dream.

I also read for the parents of a teenager who had died in a car accident. She, too, wanted to communicate that it hadn't been painful. Just to make sure I got the message, she shared the whooshing sensation she experienced as her soul left the body, straight out of the top of her head—not once or twice, but three times in a row. It didn't hurt, but it left me dizzy for a few minutes.

FACES OF THE DEAD

One of the things I inherited from my dad is a fascination with the past. Maybe that's because I was raised on a farm, where the past wasn't that far away. I grew up in North Dakota, in a house my grandfather built, on land my great-grandparents had homesteaded. We were surrounded by prairies and fields that looked the same for at least a hundred miles in any direction. The landscape was flat, and there were hardly any trees. Our view was mostly sky, but my dad always made it feel as though new sights and new adventures were all around us.

Time and time again while I was growing up, we would head into town on some errand, only to find ourselves taking a very long way home. It wasn't unusual for the five-mile drive to turn into a two- or three-hour expedition. My dad would suddenly remember long-lost uncles or neighbors or classmates, and we would start to head out to whatever part of the countryside they used to haunt. He'd find a shelter belt of trees set back from a gravel road, and then we'd turn up a long-abandoned driveway to stare at the remnants of an old barn, leaning dangerously to one side like a drunk, or walk around the crumbling stone foundation of a house that had long ago been blown away by a tornado.

Image 70: My grandparents, Esther and Walter Kenner, and my dad, Wayne, as a toddler. The buggy was antique, even in 1942, but they were taking it for a joyride on their North Dakota farm.

One afternoon when I was twelve or thirteen, my dad announced that he wanted to drive out to an old pioneer cemetery built by the Sons of Norway. My mom and two younger sisters had no interest, but I happily scampered into his boxy Jeep Wagoneer. The sun was still high in the sky when we left; it was late spring, just a month from the summer solstice, and the days were long close to the Canadian border. It was hot too; North Dakota has extreme weather, and the temperature that day had probably topped out in the upper eighties.

We drove down a two-lane highway for a few miles, not seeing any other traffic except for tractors in the fields, where farmers were planting wheat that would eventually be milled into flour for pasta. We turned off the highway and bounced along a series of rutted gravel roads. They'd been torn up by trucks and tractors driving over them through a long winter of snow and rough plowing, followed by a wet spring. My dad's four-wheel drive was great for careening over rough country roads, but it wasn't a smooth ride. Even at slow speeds, we were tossed around like sailors on a stormy sea. We had the windows open because no one had air conditioning in their vehicles back then. The wind whipped through the car, spiraling around us, occasionally blowing black dirt and bits of gravel into our faces. These days, you'd have to pay me to ride through a hailstorm of grit and debris, but back then, it was part of every drive through the countryside.

It wasn't long before we found the old cemetery near a small, one-room church. We pulled off the road, parked on the grass, and ambled in.

The cemetery was small, with maybe a hundred or two hundred tombstones. There were probably more graves there than we could tell; many of the markers were homemade, and some dated back to the 1880s. Some had names punched into tin, while others were carved into old wood, and over the years a lot of them had disintegrated. Some, of course, were traditional tombstones of marble and granite. A few of those featured old photos pressed under curved glass.

Many of the graves belonged to children and young adults. I remember being fascinated by the tombstone of a boy who died at sixteen. His photo was mounted on his monument, and it was hard to reconcile his face— alert, alive, and animated—with the thought of his remains, crumbling to dust, in the earth beneath my feet. His portrait was so compelling that it still haunts me to this day.

The photo didn't look old; it didn't seem to have aged at all in the seventy-five years since he had been buried. I knew there was probably nothing left of the boy himself. He had lived and died long before I was born. He was buried facing east, which is traditional, to await his resurrection with the rising sun.

As I stood there, I think I faced my own mortality for the first time. I thought of all the decades that face in the photo, with those clear, unblinking eyes, had been looking out across the cemetery. Month after month, year after year, through arid summers and frozen winters, he was frozen in time. As the seasons passed, the prairie grass would sprout, young and green, and then turn golden brown as summer reached the fall. As the sun rose and set, clouds and constellations would drift overhead. Approaching thunderstorms would tint the sky an eerie green; blizzards would blow with snow so heavy that the horizon would be imperceptible, and earth and sky would be bathed in the same blinding white light. I imagined his lifeless form beneath the ground but his soul behind the glass that shielded his photo from the elements. Like a fly trapped in amber, I imagined him gazing out across the prairie. I thought of him looking at the church, still standing, where he had been baptized, sang every Sunday, and was then shepherded to his final resting place.

As crazy as it sounds, I felt like I knew him. It was spooky, but some part of his soul was definitely in the cemetery that day.

I wish I could remember his name, but it was too long ago, and now the cemetery is too far away. But I do remember his face, and I remember it was the first time I started really thinking about all the stories the dead could tell, if only we knew how to listen.

AN OPEN INVITATION TO THE SPIRIT WORLD

While graveyards can be haunted, you don't need to visit a cemetery to commune with spirits. In fact, spirits will come when you call them, wherever *you* happen to be. Your great-aunt can join you at her gravesite, when you're thinking of the pies she used to bake. She can also ride along in your car, singing in the Spirit World when her favorite song comes on the radio. Ghosts aren't limited by time and space, and they're certainly not locked behind cemetery gates.

Not too long ago, a cheerful-looking woman came into the shop, accompanied by her grown daughter. She saw our tarot parlor and asked for a one-card reading.

"Can you do mediumship?" she asked. I nodded as I shuffled the cards.

"I want to know about my father. No, wait. My first husband. What can you tell me about him?"

I kind of laughed to myself, because once you call a spirit into a reading, you can't slam the door in its face and tell it to go away. In that instant, I realized the woman had summoned both men.

Image 71: Spirits often come into the Haunted Antique Shop with living visitors.

I could feel them as if they had materialized out of thin air—which, in a way, I suppose they had. It wasn't like they stormed through the door, although the effect was the same. Two strong personalities had suddenly jumped into the room, crossing the threshold as comfortably as if someone had called them in, because that's exactly what had happened.

She looked too young to be a widow, so I double-checked. "They've both passed?"

"Yes," she said. "My dad is passed, and my first husband died years ago." She sighed. "I think about him a lot."

At that moment, two cards fell out of the deck, exactly as if they had been plucked from my hand. I will say that cards normally don't come tumbling out when I shuffle. When they do, it's significant.

"Let me tell you about each card," I said, "and you can tell me which is which. The Two of Wands is a businessman, an entrepreneur. He was at the top of his game. The illustration shows a captain of industry who sent out his ships and is now waiting to see what they'll bring back to port. Is that your dad?"

She nodded.

"The Strength card shows a man who conquered his demons, who tamed his wild animal nature. And this is an infinity symbol above his head...so this must be your husband, because he's on your mind so much."

"Yes. He had a lot of demons."

"Did they have anything to do with how he died?"

"Yes, he killed himself when he was twenty-five. He had some addiction issues, some mental illness, some bipolar."

I felt her late husband's spirit agree. Oddly enough, he didn't disavow those demons.

"He says those issues weren't weaknesses. In fact, he says they're part of what made him strong. And now he's timeless."

Those thoughts weren't mine. They came from somewhere outside of me, and I relayed them as soon as I heard them. The woman was starting to get emotional, but she was able to say she understood completely.

Then there was one more message.

"He says he always thought you were beautiful. He still does."

The woman, who was crying now, could only nod. Her daughter smiled warmly and said, "It's so funny you say that, because she's always asking, 'Am I pretty?'"

I was glad to hear the message resonated. We had time for one parting thought. I like to ask spirits how they'll continue to communicate, and they offered their signs.

"Both men say they're still around you," I relayed. "Your dad, the businessman, sends money. Coins. Literally, pennies from heaven." Both women laughed, because the mother apparently has a habit of finding loose change wherever she goes. "And your husband," his spirit added, "sends red flowers."

Some of my favorite tarot readings include spirit communication. I like passing along messages from people who have died, because they comfort the people they left behind—and because I never really know what the spirits are going to say.

When living clients get spirit readings, they usually arrive a few minutes before their appointments. Their dead friends and relatives, however, sometimes show up days in advance. I often sense them as I'm getting dressed or brushing my hair or making coffee. Some ghosts have no respect for personal space.

I'm pretty sure I'm not the only medium who has to set boundaries. I do that with tarot cards. I'll even go so far as to talk out loud when I feel spirits trying to encroach on my routine. "Not yet," I say. "Wait until I get my cards out."

OUR LADY OF SLUMBER

Years ago, before I did psychic work of my own, I started collecting Virgin Mary figurines. I still collect them. I especially like the vintage porcelains that double as planters, with a compartment in the back for flowers or a houseplant. Most of them are ceramic, hand-painted in gentle pastel colors, and accented with gold. Most also date back to the 1940s, '50s, and '60s.

Some might call them kitschy, but Marian memorabilia appeals to me for two reasons: I was a convert to Catholicism, and I'm fascinated by its idealized depictions of motherhood, feminine beauty, and spiritual grace.

At first, I kept my Virgin Mary figurines wherever I had room: on bookshelves, side tables, and countertops. As my collection grew, I decided to feature it more prominently. I cleared the top of a dresser in my bedroom, laid out a doily my great-grandmother Snow had crocheted before I was born, and arranged all the Virgin Mary statues to watch over me while I slept.

I was so naïve.

That first night, I hardly slept at all. As soon as I turned out the lights and curled up in bed, the voices started.

Some were whispers. Some were murmured conversations. Most seemed to be gathered in the hallway outside my bedroom door, while a few seemed to be coming from the corners of my room.

Image 72: Ghosts are attracted to religious relics like this vintage Virgin Mary figurine.

When I talk to people who have experienced ghostly activity, a surprising number describe one fascinating aspect of their encounters: they weren't particularly frightening. Ghostly visitations are mystifying, of course—even mesmerizing. But it's more common than not to simply watch and wonder as ghosts manifest and interact around us. Hardly anyone runs screaming into the street. Most of us simply register the fact that something odd is happening, and when it ends, we get on with whatever we were doing in the first place.

That night, I laid in bed for hours, listening to the quiet hum of voices. They would stop when I turned on my bedside lamp but start again when I turned it off. After a few hours, I managed to drift off. I didn't sleep soundly, though, because the sound never stopped.

The next morning, I stopped to talk with a coworker who did psychic work on the side.

"I'm pretty sure I had ghosts in my house last night," I said.

"Did they bother you?"

"Of course, they bothered me! They talked and walked around all night long."

She looked at me, assessing. I suppose she wondered if she'd have to come to my house and do a spiritual cleansing or something.

"You've never heard anything like it before?"

I shook my head.

"That's odd that it would start up so suddenly," she said. "Has anything changed in your house? Did you buy something new? Has anyone given you a gift? Have you picked up any antiques?"

Ahh. Suddenly it all started to make sense.

"Now that you mention it," I said, "I did rearrange a collection of Virgin Mary statues. I consolidated them all in my bedroom. They look so pretty, all in a group."

She smiled.

"So you're telling me," she said, "that you set up a shrine to the Virgin Mary, the most famous saint in history, and you're surprised that spirits are drawn to it?"

I laughed. "Well, when you put it that way, I guess I did."

"It's fine," she said. "Ghosts who come to pray are good-hearted spirits. They won't hurt you. But if you hear them again, just tell them to be quiet because you need to sleep."

That night, before I went to bed, I spoke aloud to any ghosts that might have been gathering. "You're welcome to worship here," I said, "but you can't make noise. I have to work in the morning."

I still have a Virgin Mary collection on my dresser, but now it's a place for quiet contemplation, not conversation.

TRIGGER OBJECTS

In the world of paranormal investigation, some ghost hunters rely on "trigger objects" like religious figurines to attract and study spirit activity. My Virgin Mary figurines were a powerful trigger, even though it was inadvertent.

In the years since then, I've learned that spirits are drawn to the same objects that fascinated them in life. Children's ghosts like toys, especially ones they can manipulate with their limited spirit energy: dolls, stuffed animals, balls, and toy cars. Adults who smoked usually can't resist tobacco and cigarettes. Gamblers like cards and dice. Drinkers are drawn to alcohol. And Christians, even in the afterlife, are fond of holy relics.

FREE GHOST WITH PURCHASE

At the Haunted Antique Shop, some people wonder if they'll get more than they bargain for. "If I buy something here," they ask, "will a ghost follow me home?"

Image 73: The Haunted Antique Shop at twilight.

I'm never really sure how to answer. If I want to close the sale, first I have to figure out whether those customers actually *want* a free ghost with their purchase.

The truth is that spirits are attached to antiques because someone, somewhere, found them worth keeping. The antiques we see today weren't always old, but they were always treasured. Every antique was cherished, either for its financial worth or its sentimental value.

What many people don't know is that objects don't have to be old to be haunted. They simply need to be imbued with emotional energy. You could even be haunted by something you bought new at a department store if someone else was invested in it.

If an antique makes you feel good, you can simply enjoy sharing it with the generations who cared for it before you. If your possessions seem possessed, however, you can use the same steps you would take to clean an entire house to clear your belongings too. Dust them off, spritz them with holy water, ask unhappy ghosts to move on, and give them your blessing.

TEENY TINY GHOSTS

Of course, if you truly do want a ghost to follow you home, we can make that happen. We sell Teeny Tiny Ghosts at the shop, bottled in-house, and willing to accompany you wherever you might travel.

Image 74: We bottle our own line of Teeny Tiny Ghosts here at the shop.

I started making them when someone gave me hundreds of teeny tiny glass bottles. I wasn't sure what to do with them all at first, and then it hit me: there's no better way to preserve our inventory than by bottling it.

Each ghost is handcrafted, with a hand-embroidered face. I like to think that I'm simply giving form to formless spirits who want to be seen. And while I make all the ghosts the same way, each one still comes out with a slightly different expression, because each has its own unique personality.

Every Teeny Tiny Ghost comes with instructions for its care and comfort, along with an adoption certificate. The certificates are inscribed with an old-fashioned name, and I never assign the same name twice. In fact, I keep a record of all the Teeny Tiny Ghosts that fly out the door.

You probably won't be surprised to learn that the ghosts really do fly out the door. They're our best seller.

A BLESSING FROM POPE CHUCK

The card was unmistakable: a blood-red heart, frozen in mid-air, stilled by three double-edged swords. The sky was gray, and rain was falling from heavy, swollen, low-hanging clouds. I already knew the answer, but I asked anyway. "Did your husband die from a heart attack?"

Across the table, a young woman had been holding her breath. Now her eyes filled with tears, and she nodded, unable to speak. I handed her a tissue.

She wiped her eyes and tucked the used tissue into her purse.

"He was only forty," she said. "He died ten years ago."

The young widow had stopped by for a tarot reading, hoping to reconnect with her late husband. She was distraught; the pain of losing him was still as raw as it had been the first day.

I could feel his presence at the table with us. "Let's see how he wants to show himself to you," I said. I pulled the next card from the top of the deck and turned it face up.

It was the Fool. We both laughed, the tension broken, and I told her that the Fool usually describes an adventurer with a zest for life, a willingness to take risks, and someone who might leap before he looks, trusting that he'll always land on his feet.

"That was Chuck," she said. "One hundred percent."

She took a deep breath and asked the same question most people ask during spirit readings: "Is he still with me?" The next card I turned over was the Hierophant. Well, that's weird, I thought. The imposing figure, the head of a religious and spiritual hierarchy, is about as far from the Fool as you can get.

Image 75: A chalkware sculpture of the Infant of Prague raising his right hand in blessing.

"He says he's with you," I said, "and he's always giving you his blessing, just like the man in this card." I raised my hand to demonstrate the way priests use their hands to make the sign of the cross in the air. At the same time, I could see Chuck in my mind's eye, literally wearing papal regalia like a Halloween costume and laughing. "But why does he say he really is dressed like the Pope?"

She broke into a broad grin and laughed out loud.

"Why am I not surprised?" she answered. "It's because he was Catholic. I wasn't, really, but I gave him a big Catholic funeral, with a full mass and rosaries, which I knew he wanted. I took one of those rosaries home, and I've got it hanging on a crucifix above our bedroom door. Every day, I wake up and look at the cross on the wall and say, 'Good morning, Chuck,' and I just feel like we still have that moment of connection. So yeah, I can see it. I can totally see him dressed like the pope. My husband, Pope Chuck."

As a tarot reader, I look forward to spirit readings because the messages that come through the cards always leave clients feeling comforted. The readings help survivors remember their loved ones at their best, and they remind us that our loved ones continue to live on in spirit. Some of them can even leave us laughing rather than in tears.

DREAM VACATION

Occasionally, the people I've known in life come back to visit after death. My connection with them doesn't have to be particularly close. Sometimes, I've hardly known them at all, but they'll ask me to deliver messages to loved ones they left behind.

I once knew an old lawyer who had closed his practice and retired. As so often happens, he had worked well into his golden years, and by the time he wrapped up all his case files, he didn't have a long life left to enjoy. He died within months of retirement.

One night soon after he crossed over, the lawyer came to me in a dream. I was sound asleep, not worried, not anxious, and not thinking or dreaming of anything in particular.

Suddenly, I found myself fully alert in a surprisingly lucid dream. I was standing on a soft, sandy beach on a tropical shore with palm trees swaying under a clear blue sky.

The old attorney stood in front of me—still stooped, still wrinkled, and still battling bushy eyebrows that grew wild, as if he was hiding beneath them. He looked just like he had in life—but there was one major difference. In my dream, he wasn't scowling like he had been every time I'd met him. He was smiling. Beaming, even. In fact, he had the biggest, widest grin I'd ever seen on a skinny old man.

"Can you get a message to my wife?" he asked.

I shrugged. "Maybe," I said.

ST. PETERSBURG, FLA.—Fisherman's Palmetto Shack.

Image 76: A fisherman's palmetto hut in Florida, circa 1900.

"Take a look at this," he said proudly, stepping to the side and sweeping his arm out in a grand gesture. He pointed with pride to a cozy thatched hut, with a roof of woven palm fronds like you might see in a travel brochure. Off to the side, a canvas hammock was strung between two trees. A warm breeze carried the scent of tropical flowers, and I could hear the gentle percussion of waves lapping on the beach.

"I want her to know that I'm okay," he said. "In fact, I want her to know that, finally, I am on *permanent* vacation."

With that, the connection broke. My dream ended in an instant, and I woke up in the still and quiet darkness of the night.

The next morning, I mentioned the dream to my mom, who was friends with the lawyer's widow. My mom mentioned it to her later that week.

Much to my surprise, the widow wasn't saddened or shocked by the news. She didn't laugh in disbelief or deny the possibility that her husband had sent a message from beyond the grave.

In fact, she believed it completely. She had waited her whole life to retire with her husband, and when he left this world without her, she felt cheated.

That's why her reaction should have been easier to predict. She simply shook her head and muttered under her breath, "Oh, that son of a bitch."

RELATIVELY SPEAKING

Back at the start of this book, I told you how I modeled the shop after my great-grandmother's house in Minneapolis. It worked: some days when I walk into the shop, I halfway expect to see her sitting in the front room, looking out the window, making wry observations about the people passing by.

Image 77: My daughter Emily with my great-grandmother Martha Hansen.

My Grandma Hansen was a Danish immigrant who was born in 1894. She actually came to the hospital while my mother was in labor, determined to be on hand for my arrival. Years later, she was just as excited to meet my children—and she even continued to keep an eye on them after she died.

My daughter Emily has always been a good sleeper. Even when she was only a year old, she usually slept soundly through the night and didn't wake up until she heard the rest of the family moving around. Normally, I tried to keep the house quiet until her breakfast was ready at seven or eight.

Around six a.m. one morning, however, I woke to the sound of voices. I checked to see if my alarm had switched to a broadcast of some sort, but it hadn't. I checked Kate's room, which was next to mine. Everything was quiet. The voices seemed to be coming from Emily's room at the end of the hall.

Her door was shut, so before I disturbed her, I checked the rest of the house. There was no sound in the living room, the kitchen, or the basement. I now was certain the voices were coming from the baby's room.

For some reason, I didn't feel alarmed. I stood outside her door for a moment, listening. It sounded like there were five or six adults in the room: two or three women were apparently cooing at the baby, while in the background two or three men seemed to be talking among themselves. I couldn't understand what they were saying, though, because they were speaking some sort of Scandinavian language.

Suddenly, it dawned on me: My great-grandmother had died just a few weeks before at the age of ninety-nine. She had emigrated from Denmark as a young woman and had never seen most of her thirteen brothers and sisters again. I simply knew that she had come back to see the baby—and to show her off to some of her long-lost relatives.

After a moment, I reached out to open the door and just as my hand touched the knob, the voices stopped. I peeked in, and Emily was standing in her crib, wide awake, staring into the middle of the room. She was too young to tell me what she had seen—but after that, the voices returned several times. I don't mind. I know it's Grandma stopping in to check on us.

DESTINY'S DOORKNOB

There's a doorknob in the Cabinet of Curiosities with glass handles that sparkle like diamonds. The brass plates are tarnished, and traces of white paint highlight their art deco design. It's at least a hundred years old, and everyone who holds it notices its weight. When you come to the Haunted

Antique Shop, try picking it up for yourself; you'll see that it feels heavy and substantial in the palm of your hand.

Image 78: Psychometry can help you open doorways to psychic experience.

What doors did it open? What secrets did it guard?

Imagine yourself standing before a paneled door, turning the knob gently. Envision the door swinging open and picture the room you might have entered.

I did, and here's what I saw:

I found myself in an old-fashioned bedroom with high ceilings and wallpaper in green and white stripes. It was furnished with a canopied four-poster bed, a dressing table and chair, and an oversized round mirror.

A young woman sat at the dressing table. I could see her reflection as she brushed her hair. She wore a long gown with a high collar and a full skirt that gathered at her waist and pooled at her feet.

Around her, like a film playing in fast-forward, children crawled on the floor, then scampered at her knee, then grew tall and walked away.

A man stood in the corner, watching her with a fond expression on his face. He, too, grew older, then faded away.

She seemed young at first, but as I watched, she aged. Her complexion started smooth, then grew careworn and lined. With time, her hair faded from a rich and glossy auburn to platinum white.

There were windows behind her, framed with lace curtains. Through panes of lead glass, I could see the sun rise and set, the moon rise and fall, and constellations spinning through the night. By day, clouds rolled across blue skies. By night, the moon cycled through its phases, over and over, again and again. It waxed to full, then waned to black. A young oak grew taller, sending its branches soaring toward heaven. Small buds sprouted in the rain, and green leaves grew toward the sun. They danced and shimmered in the breeze, then turned brown and fell to the ground.

Day after day, night after night, the woman sat at her dressing table, brushing her hair. Every morning, she pinned it up. Every evening, she plaited it into a braid.

Sometimes she smoothed the curls on her forehead as she studied the lines that grew deeper and more numerous on her face. Sometimes she smiled. Sometimes she wiped tears from her eyes.

At long last, she rose, standing feebly, and took one last look in the mirror. The sun was setting. She turned down the blankets and climbed into bed. Darkness fell, the moon rose, and stars gleamed in the night sky. As my vision faded, she closed her eyes and fell asleep.

CHAPTER 6

SPIRIT COMMUNICATION

Sometimes people come in and say they can't reconcile the concept of ghosts with their religious beliefs. Sometimes, they even tell me point-blank that they don't believe in what I do—as if the sign outside the shop was also an invitation to come in and challenge my life choices.

Those types of comments used to throw me for a loop. How was I supposed to respond?

Initially, I felt a little defensive, as if I had to justify my work, and I worried that they were looking for a fight. With time, however, I've learned that people who open with denials are actually trying to make a completely different point. These days, I simply wait for the big revelation that's almost sure to follow.

With a quick, furtive glance to make sure no one else is around, and a few tentative words to make sure I won't call them crazy, those visitors start to open up.

They tell me how they grew up in a house where spirits walked through walls. They describe how their grandfather's ghost used to tuck them in at night. They talk about birds and butterflies they know were sent by those they loved and phone calls from disconnected numbers.

They're not alone. In 2018, a Chapman University survey revealed that 57 percent of Americans believe that some places can be haunted by spirits.

Another survey found that more than sixty percent of people have seen a ghost—and more than forty percent claim their pet has seen one too.

Image 79: This papier-mâché angel hangs above the doorway of our tarot parlor.

Their stories align perfectly with religious and theological tradition.

Christianity is founded on the belief that the human soul is eternal and that Jesus Christ fulfilled God's promise of everlasting life. Catholics believe that we can and should pray for the souls of the dead. And in some cases, Catholic theologians say those souls can appear to us in return.

Saint Thomas Aquinas wrote that it is "absurd to say souls of the departed do not leave their abode ... according to the disposition of divine providence, separated souls sometimes come forth from their abode and appear to men." Saint Thomas himself believed that he was visited by the ghosts of his sister and a former Dominican brother.

Some denominations believe that ghosts are souls who linger on earth before they continue their journey to heaven. In those cases, they believe that God allows them to appear in order to ask for prayers and remind the living to guard the state of their own souls.

Many churchgoers also believe that spirits of the dead can return to bring them comfort. It makes sense. If the saints and the souls of the faithful departed can intercede for us, why wouldn't God allow them to reveal their ongoing presence in our lives?

WHY DO SPIRITS LINGER?

If you grew up on a steady diet of ghost stories, as I did, you probably grew up believing that ghosts and spirits linger on this plane for dramatic reasons—including power, revenge, and unfinished business. The hotel ghosts in *The Shining*, for example, wanted to feed off the energy of the living. *The Woman in Black* wanted vengeance for the son she lost. Patrick Swayze's *Ghost* remained earthbound to protect Demi Moore until his murderers were no longer a threat.

While those narratives are the stuff of compelling books and movies, they're not exactly common. It's possible that some ghosts have unfinished business or find themselves trapped on the earth plane by trauma and confusion surrounding their deaths. Some could avoid crossing over because of guilt, fear, or anger.

That hasn't been my experience, though. Many of them have shown me their lives in the Spirit World, and they seem content.

That's because ghosts are people too. They have the same motivations we do. We want to love and be loved, protect the people we care about, and pursue our shared interests. Most of us aren't evil masterminds, determined to destroy our enemies and accumulate power at all costs. Even the worst people we meet are usually more misguided than malevolent.

Most spirits linger on this plane for wholesome reasons. They return to reassure their loved ones that life goes on, even after death. They come to comfort those who are grieving and console those they've left behind. They cross the veil to reconnect while they wait for a more permanent reunion.

THE SPECTRAL SPECTRUM

What do you picture when you think of a ghost? A wisp of smoke? A glowing orb? A transparent human figure?

Image 80: A 1904 reunion of some of DeLand's original settlers and their descendants. Henry DeLand is the man with the long white beard seated in the center.

You'd be right on all counts. Ghosts are energy, and that energy can take many forms.

What do ghosts look like? For centuries, people who have seen ghosts and spirits have also described several common features.

SENTIENT SPIRITS

First and foremost, ghosts can look just like they did in life. Sometimes, they're transparent, or their legs and feet seem to fade away to nothing. Either way, full-body apparitions look a lot like living people.

Some ghosts are misty, like a fog. They can materialize into something more solid, taking human form before your very eyes. Others look like swirling funnels and wispy spirals of light. The ectoplasmic apparitions sometimes only show in photos, and they're especially common around old houses, graveyards, battlefields, and other historic sites.

Some spirits take the form of orbs—transparent, translucent, glowing balls of blue or white light. Orbs can hover in place or move like lightning. Some people believe orbs can be ghosts, but they can also be portals between this world and the next.

You probably won't be surprised to learn that the Haunted Antique Shop has more than its share of orbs. An amateur ghost hunter named Vance visited the shop after dark one night, hoping to capture a few orbs on video. He found hundreds of them, dancing and spinning like fireworks—especially in the tarot parlor.

Ghostly apparitions aren't limited to human spirits, either. Many people report that animals who have crossed the rainbow bridge can and do return. When spectral pets visit, their former owners often hear a familiar scratching at the door, tiny paws padding across the floor, or a familiar weight curling up at the foot of their bed.

NON-SENTIENT SPIRITS

Then again, some ghosts aren't really ghosts at all—at least, not in the conventional sense of the word. Non-sentient spirits operate without awareness, and they don't interact with the living.

Some ghosts are merely residual imprints of strong emotions, echoing across the landscape of time and space. Strong emotional energy can be permanently etched in place to be played back at certain times of the day or the year. People who report seeing ghostly students in old schools, for example, are often seeing residual ghosts. The same can be said about people who hear weeping in graveyards, music in empty concert halls, or laughter in vacant rooms. Residual ghosts don't interact with the living. They're not conscious of their surroundings. They're merely shadowy remnants of the past.

Some ghosts are thought forms, inadvertently willed into existence by collective expectations and experience. Take the ghost of Bloody Mary, for example. She's been called forth at thousands of slumber parties. That doesn't mean she actually originated as a real girl, in real life, or that she has enough power to do more than frighten giddy teenagers. Instead, the ghost of Bloody Mary is an example of focused energy and excitement that has taken on a life of its own.

Throughout human history, we've all shared stories, myths, and legends. When we put enough spiritual, emotional, and intellectual energy into an imaginary creation, it can manifest in the material world, too, as a thought form.

Some call those thought forms *egregores*, from a Greek word that means "wakeful." Others have adapted that word, calling composite ghosts *aggregates*. That describes the psychic energy that accumulates as more people channel their energy into an idea. People who belong to magical groups create egregores on purpose, but other people, knowingly or not, can create them too. It's possible that anyone who expects a supernatural experience can manifest one, even if they're creating it on a subconscious level.

In addition to residual hauntings and thought forms, a third type of non-sentient spirit could result from glitches in the matrix of time and space. While it sounds like science fiction, some ghosts could be glimpses of other selves in a parallel reality. That could also explain reports of doppelgängers, which are mysterious apparitions of living people. Doppelgängers often don't respond to friendly waves or greetings, as if they don't even see us in this world. It could be that they don't see us because they're not with us. They're actually on a different plane in another dimension. If that's the case, we might look like ghosts in their world too.

SPIRIT BEINGS

Some ghostly entities have never lived a mortal existence.

Spirit guides, for example, are cosmic entities who might have had lives on earth—but that's not always the case. Some have never incarnated as earthly beings in physical form. Even so, they're a constant presence in our lives, reminding us of our purpose and helping us achieve our full potential.

Many people feel a close connection with guardian angels, who are credited with saving us from harm, leading us to safety, and guiding us to success. In many religious traditions, angels also serve as heavenly messengers and intermediaries.

Demons, on the other hand, are fallen angels, perpetually trying to sow seeds of chaos, confusion, and fear in an ongoing war of rebellion against God and revenge against mankind.

While poltergeists might seem demonic, they're actually strong negative emotions that manifest as disruptive, violent energy. Poltergeists aren't demons, though, and they're not ghosts. They're the physical manifestations of fear and distress.

Elemental creatures, like fairies, sylphs, elves, gnomes, salamanders, and undines, are personifications of the ancient forces of earth, fire, air, and water. From time immemorial, they've been part of our history, mystery, legend, and lore. Some elemental creatures can mimic human voices and actions, and they can harness their supernatural powers to help or hinder the living.

GHOSTS AND SPIRITS

Most of the ghosts at the Haunted Antique Shop are intelligent and interactive. They're the souls of people who died, and they know they're dead. They know the circumstances of their death. They can respond to questions, react to physical objects, and communicate with the living. In short, ghosts are people too.

No matter what type of ghost you happen to encounter, it's best to treat them with dignity and respect—just as you would treat any other person, corporeal or not. For a guide to ghostly etiquette, read on.

"MIST" MANNERS

Most ghosts are like most people. Some are outgoing. Some are reserved. As a rule, they're friendly and approachable, but they can also be quiet and soft-spoken. The circumstances of their existence don't give them much choice in that department. And while they can be playful, they're almost never harmful or malicious—at least without a reason.

Image 81: Early photographers tried to capture spirit interaction on film. Some resorted to double exposures.

The next time you find yourself face-to-face with a ghost, remember these simple rules of social interaction on every plane of existence:

- Try to treat ghosts just as you would treat the living. Talk to a ghost as you would talk to a friend, a neighbor, or someone you've just met.

- Be polite. Introduce yourself. Ask questions and listen patiently for the answers, which may come in the form of subtle signs and symbols.

- While you're learning how to communicate with a ghost, try using tools and technology to help you communicate. Pendulums and dowsing rods are fun and easy to use, and they're remarkably effective.

- When you get a response from a ghost, acknowledge it and thank them for interacting with you. Most experts agree that it takes a lot of spiritual energy to cross the divide between this world and the next, and it's worth a word of appreciation.

- If you invite a spirit to communicate, don't be surprised if they respond—and don't scream or run away. Imagine inviting a friend for coffee. Would you be alarmed if they showed up at your doorstep? Would you shriek and slam the door?

- On the other hand, if you have uninvited contact from a ghost, it's perfectly proper to ask them to leave you alone.

- Recognize that ghosts aren't necessarily lost souls. Many have seen the light, crossed over, and then returned to this plane of existence out of genuine fondness for the living.

- Treat ghosts with dignity and respect. Remember that most of them are older than you. They have life and death experiences that transcend your own.

- Most ghosts are veiled, not jailed. They're free to come and go at will.

- Speak kindly. If you insult, demean, or denigrate ghosts, they won't respond. If you treat them poorly, they'll move on to a better place. Don't be surprised if they disappear completely.

- You can invite a ghost to communicate, but you can't command or compel one to do your bidding.

A SURVEY OF PSYCHIC SKILLS

Psychic skills aren't limited to a few gifted soothsayers. Psychic ability is as natural as breathing.

Psychic talents are grounded in empathy, instinct, and intuition—all basic skills for human survival. Those gifts aren't always valued, however, especially in a society that prizes logic and objectivity. When psychic capabilities are undermined and ignored, they're not cultivated or developed, either.

The next time you see, hear, or feel something unusual, don't disregard a supernatural explanation. Your psychic senses might be trying to tell you something important—and you might be surprised to discover that you have psychic gifts and talents you've never recognized.

Image 82: DeLand's main street, Woodland Boulevard, during the days of the Model T.

You've probably heard of precognition. The word itself is literally a variation of "pre-recognition." It's the ability to know the future and see events before they occur. Empathy is the ability to feel, sense, and understand emotions that aren't your own, and telepathy is the ability to tune in to other people's thoughts.

Other psychic gifts are simply an extension of your other five senses: sight, sound, smell, taste, and touch.

- Sight: *clairvoyance* is "clear vision." You might see ghosts and apparitions as if they're standing in front of you. You might be able to see them clearly in your mind's eye. You might also be able to see the images and symbols they transmit.
- Sound: *clairaudience* is "clear hearing." It's the ability to hear audible messages from the Spirit World. You might hear ghostly voices, loud and clear, as if they're standing next to you. Alternately, words, phrases, and sentences could simply pop into your head.

- Smell: I use the word *clairarôme* to describe "clear aroma." Others call the skill *clairalience*. It's a gift that's so important—and so overlooked—that it deserves its own discussion. Read on for details.
- Taste: *clairgustance* means "clear taste." Ghosts and spirits sometimes transmit the memory of favorite flavors they loved in life, like strawberries, mint, or chocolate.
- Touch: *clairsentience* is French for "clear sensing." Clairsentience can feel like impressions or gut feelings, sudden flashes of insight, or a clear understanding of other people's motivations or desires. If you're clairsentient, sometimes spirits will allow you to feel what they felt as they died. You might experience subtle variations of their physical symptoms, like headaches or chest pain.

SCENT BY SPIRIT

Of all the "clairs," *clairarôme* is the most common—and the least frightening.

Why? Because we're almost never prepared to come face-to-face with a full-fledged, full-body apparition. Disembodied voices will send most people running. And symbolic mental imagery, delivered telepathically, can easily be misconstrued.

Scent, however, is unmistakable, and it's usually linked to happy memories. Scientifically, scent is the strongest, surest link to memory and emotion. The sense of smell is intertwined with the memory centers of the brain.

A hint of perfume in the air can be as comforting as a mother's hug, and the aroma of pipe tobacco can be a warm reminder of a favorite uncle. A long-forgotten scent can even bring people to tears, unleashing memories that would otherwise never be recalled.

Ghosts know that revealing themselves through scent will reopen their connections to the living. Try it for yourself right now: imagine the smell of freshly cut grass, smoke drifting over a campfire, or coffee brewing in your grandmother's kitchen. Where do those smells take you? Close your eyes, remember those aromas, and you'll find yourself in another place and time.

You might even find yourself reconnecting with a ghost from your past.

MORPHEUS, HYPNOS, AND THANATOS

For thousands of years, people have known that dreams connect us to the Other Side. In ancient Greece, Morpheus was the god of dreams, Hypnos was the god of sleep, and his twin brother, Thanatos was the god of peaceful death.

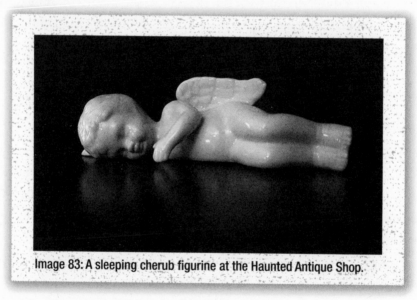

Image 83: A sleeping cherub figurine at the Haunted Antique Shop.

We don't acknowledge the old gods like we used to, but they still resonate. We understand, on an intuitive level, the roles they play.

Late at night, when we're quiet and relaxed, the boundaries soften between this world and the next. Bright lights and distractions fade from view. The rush and rhythm of daily life recedes, and our rational, analytical minds can take a break. That's why we're far more open to spirit contact at night—especially when we're asleep.

Whether we travel to the astral plane to join spirits or they pop into our reality, we find ourselves in the same place and the same timeless infinity.

Sometimes, ghosts come to us before we even know they're gone. My mother, for example, had a vivid dream of a lifelong friend back in the neighborhood where she had grown up. "I dreamed about Mrs. Grahn," she told me later. "We were standing at the bus stop on the corner, and she looked at me and said, 'Well, my bus is here. It's time for me to go.'

"I was so sad when I woke up," she said, "and I thought, how silly. It was just a bus ride. But then the phone rang, and I found out Mrs. Grahn had died during the night."

The connection works both ways. You don't have to wait for a visit: you can initiate spirit contact simply by inviting your loved ones to join you in your dreams. I think of it like seeding the clouds so thoughts and ideas can coalesce.

For what it's worth, I do the same thing when I write. I simply welcome historical figures and fictional characters alike to step into my dreams overnight.

The only danger is forgetting what they've said when you wake up. Keep a notebook and a pen by your bed so you can write down your dreams as soon as your eyes open. You can also use your phone to dictate a voice memo of everything you remember.

HOW TO HUNT FOR GHOSTS

You don't need to wait for ghosts to come to you. You don't even need to invite ghosts into your space. A lot of our customers like to embark on ghost-hunting expeditions, which is a perfectly fine way to explore the Spirit World.

If you're brand-new to ghost hunting, at the Haunted Antique Shop or at any other location, start with this step-by-step guide.

- Get permission. At our shop, it's not a problem to have one or two people conduct an impromptu investigation. If you're part of a larger team or if you'd like to do a more extensive search, you can come in after hours. But if you're planning to go ghost hunting anywhere else, make sure you have the property owner's permission.

- Walk through the area to get a feel for the space. If you're planning to investigate at night, scout your location during the day.

Image 84: "The Haunted Lane," a stereoscopic image from 1889.

- Research the site by talking to the owners, reading up on the history of the site, or visiting libraries and history centers.

- Once you're in position, find something that intrigues you or a location that calls to you. Stand or sit quietly while you tune in to the energy of the space.

- Clear your mind and breathe deeply to calm and center yourself.

- State your intention or say a prayer of protection and guidance before you start.

- Don't barge in with cameras firing and electrical equipment blasting. Introduce yourself to any spirits that might be present and tell them why you're there. Invite them to communicate with you. Be specific: you can ask them to answer by speaking on tape or moving your pendulum or dowsing rods.

- As you investigate, take note of anything unusual you observe, even if it's just a feeling or impression. Pay attention to cold spots, strange noises, or movement in the corners of your eyes.

- Follow your instincts, especially if you feel moved to take photos or make recordings.

- Thank the spirits for their interactions and end with a closing prayer.

- Always leave the location as you found it.

- Summarize your observations by making notes of everything you experience.

TOOLS OF THE TRADE

Two young men walked into the shop the other day, talking to each other in low tones, vibrating with nervous energy. They looked around for a minute, then stepped up to the front desk with a question. They whispered, as if they were asking for illegal contraband.

"Do you sell ghost-hunting tools?"

As it turns out, the young men had driven over from Daytona Beach on a last-minute quest. They thought their house was haunted, and they'd invited a group of friends over to investigate that night.

I showed them the ghost-hunting kit we keep near our front entrance. Some of the tools are high-tech. We've got a couple of EMF meters, for example, that measure electromagnetic fields around objects. There's a spirit radio that quickly scans the AM/FM radio dial so ghosts can pluck the words they need out of the air. We have a voice recorder, which we use to capture spirit voices on tape—also known as EVPs, which stands for electronic voice phenomena. When you visit, you're welcome to borrow any of those tools and try your hand at ghost hunting here in the shop. We also invite you to take photos and study them for ghostly orbs or shadows.

We specialize in antiques, though—which means we get the best results with old-fashioned technology. The most popular tools in our ghost-hunting kit are the most traditional ones: pendulums and dowsing rods. The two young men were able to use them with very little training.

Image 85: Our ghost-hunting kit combines old tools and new technology. You'll also find framed photos of Henry and Sarah DeLand in the shop.

Once you open a channel of communication and connect telepathically with a ghost, the tool becomes a tuner that links your minds together. You'll hear snippets of thought, words, suggestions, and feelings—like hearing a thought that's not your own.

SPIRIT KEY PENDULUMS

Most pendulums are simply weighted objects on a string. At the shop, I make Spirit Key pendulums from skeleton keys, charms, and miniature crystal balls. Some of them can be worn as bracelets or necklaces, which was one of our customers' most frequent requests.

Traditionally, people made improvised pendulums by tying a wedding ring to a piece of string or a single strand of hair and dangling it over a woman's pregnant form to determine the sex of an unborn child. You can easily craft your own pendulum by suspending a key, pendant, or crystal from a piece of string, ribbon, or chain.

You can use a pendulum to tap into your own intuition or to communicate with the Spirit World. Either way, pendulums are easy to use. Simply rest your elbow on a table or hold your arm out horizontally. Tuck your elbow close to your side to steady yourself. Hold one end of the pendulum between your thumb and index finger and let the rest hang straight down.

Make sure the pendulum is motionless and then ask it to show you which direction it will move for yes or no. Say, "Show me 'yes'" and "Show me 'no.'"

Image 86: Spirit Key pendulums offer an easy way to talk to spirits.

As if by magic, your pendulum will start to move. Experiment until you know how your pendulum will respond to your inquiries. Commonly, a pendulum will indicate its response in one of several ways:

- Yes: up and down, like someone nodding his head up and down
- No: back and forth, like someone shaking her head no from side to side
- Maybe: a diagonal swing, from the lower left to the upper right
- I don't want to say: no movement
- Probably: a clockwise circle
- Probably not: a counterclockwise circle
- Bobble/dance: usually a yes

Pendulums can even point to answers on maps, charts, and notes. Try suspending your pendulum over a piece of paper with the words "yes" on one side, "no" on the other, and "maybe" written in the middle. Sketch a twelve-hour clock to find an auspicious time of day or use a calendar for choosing special dates. If you're looking for lost objects, hold your pendulum over a map or diagram of the area you're searching.

If you're using a pendulum to speak to spirits, ask them to move your pendulum in response to your questions or to stop its motion if it's already swinging.

DOWSING RODS

Dowsing rods, also known as divining rods, are heavy copper wire bent into an L shape. If you have a heavy-duty wire cutter, you can make them out of metal clothes hangers. The shorter side should be four to six inches long, while the longer end can range from six to twelve inches.

They're easy to use. Take one in each hand, loosely, so they can move freely. Hold them almost parallel to the floor, pointing down ever so slightly. Tuck your elbows in to steady yourself. Ask your tools to show you how they'll move for yes or no. Dowsing rods might cross, uncross, or sway to one side or the other.

Introduce yourself and then ask if any nearby spirits would like to communicate. When the rods start to move, you can ask them to spin, cross, or uncross in response to your questions. You can also ask spirits to lead you to interesting artifacts by pointing the rods in the direction you should walk. If the rods suddenly cross over each other, stop. The X marks the spot where spirit energy is strongest.

TABLE TIPPING

Small wooden tables can work like oversized pendulums. You'll probably need a friend or two to help you get started. Simply sit down around the table, place your fingertips lightly on the tabletop, and ask it to tip or move from side to side in response to yes-or-no questions. You could also ask for knocking or rapping sounds in response to your questions.

CANDLELIGHT

In a similar light, you can get good results from asking ghosts and spirits to move a candle flame right for yes, left for no.

MULTIMEDIA GHOST HUNTING

It's fun to combine old methodology with new technology. While you work with pendulums, dowsing rods, tables, or candles, have a friend measure electrical energy with an EMF meter. If you record your dowsing sessions, you might get spirit voices on tape too.

OUIJA BOARDS: YES OR NO?

You might notice that all of these tools seem to work like Ouija boards. You're right; they do. Personally, however, I think Ouija boards come with too much baggage. They've been used and misused for so long that they've become a portal for fear, not enlightenment.

Do you remember how we talked about thought forms, back in the section on types of ghosts? I think Ouija boards attract thought forms like crazy. They become more than the sum of their parts. In and of themselves, I don't think they're inherently dangerous. I just don't like all the etheric strings that are attached.

DREAM A LITTLE DREAM OF ME

Before I started making Spirit Key pendulums, I collected skeleton keys for a few years. When I started, I wasn't sure what I would do with them. I just threw them in a plastic bag with the rest of my craft supplies.

Image 87: Spirit Keys truly do unlock cosmic doorways.

I didn't know that the keys were holding on to a power that demanded to be used.

One night I pulled them out and showed them to my husband, describing how I planned to use them for necklaces and pendulums. He nodded and made a few appropriate noises of approval, as husbands do. Then I put the keys down on my nightstand, and we both went to sleep...until about three a.m. Suddenly, we were both wide awake.

"I was having the weirdest dream about those keys," I said. "It was like the keys were alive, and I was walking down a long hallway, opening doors."

He didn't answer me at first. When he did, I was stunned.

"Corrine," he said, "I was having the same dream."

That was too spooky, even for me. I turned on the lights, and we put the keys in our closet for the rest of the night.

HIGH-TECH TECHNOLOGY

Sometimes, you can get spirits to speak to you directly—especially if you use a digital recorder. You might even get good results with an audio recorder on your phone.

Ghosts find it easier to talk on tape than to make themselves heard in ordinary conversation. Spirit voices on tape are known as EVPs, which stands for electronic voice phenomena. Typically, researchers ask questions in a quiet room. When the tapes are played back, spirit voices are audible.

Make sure you have fresh batteries or a fully charged device. Turn off radios, televisions, stereos, and speakers, and ask everyone to be as quiet as possible, even if they're in other parts of the building.

Start by noting the time, date, and your location on your recording. Introduce yourself and tell the spirits that you're trying to communicate. Ask questions and give the spirits time to answer. Wait at least ten seconds between questions.

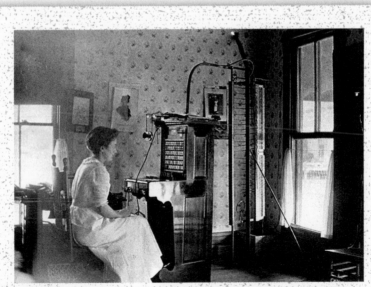

Image 88: A woman at a telephone switchboard in Central Florida, circa 1910.

If anybody makes a noise during the recording, mention it on tape. If you hear noises you can identify, describe them too. That way, you'll know the difference between normal and paranormal sounds later.

Do be specific in your requests. We learned that lesson the first time we tried recording an EVP.

"Hello," we said. "We just wanted to let you know that we hope you like what we've done with the house, and we're here to help you, if we can."

The reply, rather than giving us information, actually asked us to be more specific. When we played the tape back, we heard just one single word: a ghostly voice that asked, "How?"

We laughed when we heard it. How could we help the ghosts at the Haunted Antique Shop? We actually hadn't thought that far ahead. The ghost's response was a gentle reminder to be clear when we communicate with the unseen world. We also realized we had to be more specific in what we were willing to offer to any spirit, sight unseen.

HOW TO TALK TO SPIRITS

The dowsing process, with pendulums, rods, tables, or candles, is quick and easy to learn. You can get great results on your first try, and you'll only get better with practice.

Start by centering yourself with a few deep breaths. Introduce yourself and invite a spirit to speak with you. If you'd like to speak to someone you knew in life, call on them by name.

Now determine who you're speaking with—man, woman, or child. Get their name. They can spell it out, responding yes or no as you go through the alphabet. Ask when they lived, first by century, then by decade. Ask how they died—illness, accident, or old age.

Here are some questions you can use as a starting point:

- Is there anyone here?
- Would you like to talk to us?

Image 89: You can communicate with spirits. Just reach out: operators are standing by.

- What is your name? (You can work your way through the alphabet, but names are both personal and powerful, so you might literally hear a response or get a psychic impression.)
- Are you a man? A woman? A boy? A girl?
- Narrow down the spirit's age: Are you older than twenty? Thirty? Forty?
- Ask when the spirit lived, first by century, then by decade: Were you born during the 1900s? 1800s? The '40s? '50s? '60s?
- Did you used to live here?
- Were you married? Did you have children?
- Did you work indoors? Outdoors? In a store? An office? A factory? A farm?
- Did you die of old age? Illness? An accident?
- Is anyone else with you?
- Is there something you'd like to show us?
- Do you have a message for us?

While the question-and-answer process might seem tedious, in reality the answers will probably flow quickly. You might even hear them telepathically before you can finish asking the questions.

TIPPING THE TABLES

Not long ago, three members of a ghost hunting group—Terri, Earl, and Marie—came to the shop to look for spirit activity.

I watched, fascinated, as they used tools and technology to scan the shop. They started with EMF meters and verified that some inanimate objects were emitting tons of electromagnetic energy. They set up a laser grid that could detect shadows and movement in empty rooms, but as far as I know, they didn't catch any ghosts in the process of walking around the shop. They demonstrated a spirit box, about the size of an old-fashioned transistor radio, that could convert electromagnetic bursts into words on a digital display.

Image 90: A séance scene from the 1922 film *Dr. Mabuse the Gambler.*

After they finished surveying the shop with their electronic devices, they started describing a much older practice for spirit contact: table tipping. They brought in a small table and offered to demonstrate.

That's when the real ghost adventures started happening.

We went into my office, dimmed the lights, and all sat with our fingertips resting lightly on the tabletop. Marie knocked on the table three times, ceremoniously. In a hushed voice, she asked if any spirits would like to come in with a message.

The table started to creak and make clicking noises, as if the wood were expanding and contracting. We could feel it trembling at first, as if it were building up energy. Then it started to sway, rocking back and forth, its movement growing stronger every time it tipped from side to side. We were still simply resting our fingertips on its surface, but it felt like the table was made of rubber.

Marie talked to the table as if it was a person. "Do you have a message for one of us?" The table lurched and tilted toward Terri.

"Did you know Terri in life?" she asked. Terri, her eyes opened wide, answered for the table.

"It's my dad," she said, and the table lurched toward her.

Now Terri took over the questioning.

"Do you have something to show me?" she asked. Again, the table tipped, unmistakable in its response. "Is it in this room?" The table stood still. "Is there something outside of this room?" The table tilted toward the front room, almost as if it wanted us to follow.

We stood up, bending and stooping to keep our fingertips on the table as it skated across the room. It looked like we were sliding a giant planchette—which, come to think of it, we were. We walked backward through the doorway, and the table and Terri followed. The table led us straight to the Cabinet of Curiosities, then stopped moving.

Terri asked if there was something we should look for inside the cabinet, and the table tipped. She opened the doors, and at that point, the spirit box radio we'd almost forgotten started beeping.

Earl pointed out that the digital device was flashing two words: "case" and "son." What did it mean? Terri started looking through the items on the shelves, looking for something with a sun. She stopped when she found a vintage compact—a gold case that once held pressed powder. It was gold, with a five-pointed star on the lid.

"Well, that's a Masonic symbol," I said. "Does the word 'son' refer to the Masons, or is it a pun, because the sun is a star?"

"I'm not sure," Terri said, "but my dad was a Mason."

As it turned out, the compact's design wasn't merely Masonic. It was the emblem of the Order of the Eastern Star, an auxiliary group for the wives and daughters of Masons.

Terri put her fingertips back on the tabletop and asked, "Do you think I should have this?" The table jumped off the floor in response.

"I want it," she said, holding the compact in both hands. "It's a gift from my dad! This is going home with me."

PUNNY BUSINESS

Ghosts and spirits communicate as best they can, but they have to make do with the resources they have at hand. Sometimes, like Terri's dad, they have to resort to puns and wordplay. We might see the word "son," for example, when a spirit means "sun," or even "star." We could see the image of a lion when someone is *lying*. A goat could be a kid, a rock could be a diamond, and blue could be an emotion.

If you're seeing or hearing something that doesn't quite make sense, say it out loud or reach for different words that mean the same thing. Be flexible when you try to interpret messages from the Spirit World. Not everything you see or hear is literal. And be warned: even after death, some dads still make dad jokes.

HISTORY IN THE PALM OF YOUR HAND

Unless you're fortunate enough to inherit a family heirloom, it's almost impossible to know the full history of any antique. Most of the collectibles we sell at the Haunted Antique Shop come from estate sales, garage sales, and auctions, with no backstory.

When you hold a treasured antique, however, you can get a sense of its history—even if you know nothing about its past. Psychic energy clings to objects that were beautiful, useful, and loved by their former owners. When you tap into the psychic energy that surrounds inanimate objects, you're actually utilizing a psychic technique called psychometry.

Image 91: Antiques are often imbued with the energy of their former owners.

You've probably done it yourself without realizing you were tapping into your sixth sense. Have you ever held something that made you think of someone—or something—you once cherished? Have you ever gotten a weird vibe from an old photo, a leather-bound book, or a secondhand souvenir you picked up at a thrift shop?

Inanimate objects aren't lifeless. Items that are truly loved are imbued with positive energy. It could be that they're part of a quantum physics force field that retains energy on a quantum level. It might be that they're tools that serve as a way for spirits to communicate with us. Either way, psychometry can help you tune in to those transmissions.

Psychometry isn't just an exercise in psychic ability. It's also an exercise in meditation and imagination. It's a harmless way to test your extrasensory abilities and learn to trust your intuition. It's also a skill that can be learned, refined, and mastered, and an antique shop is the perfect place to practice.

Start with objects that would have been worn regularly, like rings and watches, or something that would have been carried in a pocket or touched often, like an old key.

- Find a quiet place. Center yourself with a few deep breaths. State your purpose, either aloud or quietly to yourself, to clarify your intention.

- Look carefully at the object you've chosen. Study it from every angle. Turn it over in your hands or try it on for size.

- Let your mind wander. Imagine how it might have been used or handled by its former owner.

- Relax and let impressions come to you. Don't try to control what happens.

- Your impressions might start slowly at first. For me, they sometimes start with glimmers of light or geometric shapes. I was holding a photo once, and all I could picture was a triangle. As it turns out, the people in the photo were in a love triangle.

- You might see images in your mind's eye, hear sounds, or pick up on phantom smells and flavors. Don't judge your impressions. Go with the flow.

- If you're using psychometry to make spirit contact, ghosts and spirits might show you symbols and images from your own life experience.

- Once you've channeled as much information as you like, thank the Spirit World for letting you peer beyond the veil.

MESSAGES FROM BEYOND

Ghosts will draw your attention to signs that are easy and accessible. They often send messages while our guard is down—when we're going about our ordinary business, focused on our own issues, and not distracted by outside cares and concerns.

Image 92: DeLand's former messenger boys can still deliver greetings from the afterlife.

Think about everything you see and hear during the course of a normal day. Over the course of a ten-minute commute to work, you could easily notice hundreds of people, places, and things. In the process, every encounter could be an opportunity for spirit contact.

At first, you might not notice subtle messages from spirit. Don't worry. They'll keep reaching out. Once you're tuned in, you'll be reminded of them as often as you like.

Here are some of the most common methods spirits use to communicate with the living:

- Birds, butterflies, and dragonflies seem to flutter by more often after a loved one dies. Countless people have told me that they notice repeated visits from winged messengers. As they defy gravity, they also defy death. Like magical creatures, they fly between worlds, transcending the limits of time and space. They remind us of angels, which makes them the most recognizable ambassadors of the Spirit World.

- Coins can be tokens of affection sent from heaven, especially if you routinely find the same type of coin—pennies, nickels, or dimes—over and over again.

- Flowers are tangible tokens of affection. Heaven-sent flowers are even more impressive if you happen to spot them growing out of season or if you stumble across them growing in unexpected places, like asphalt parking lots.

- Lucky numbers can pop up everywhere you look, and spirits often put them in our path. You might notice them on random license plates, digital clocks, street signs, and receipts. Those numbers could remind you of significant birthdates, anniversaries, or former addresses where you lived with the ones you've lost.

- Rainbows seem to materialize far more often when spirits are reaching out. They don't just appear after rainstorms. They also shimmer in prisms and fleeting reflections.

- Scents and aromas that have no apparent origin are often physical manifestations of a spirit visit. If you smell your grandmother's perfume when you're home alone, say hello to her.

- Signs and slogans sometimes offer eerily specific answers to questions you pose aloud. Billboards, commercials, and print ads can suddenly appear before you as if they're directly responding to a question you've just asked. Even signs you misread or comments you mishear could be a spirit's way of giving you the direction you need.

- Snippets of overheard conversations can also be communication from the Spirit World. We've all had the experience of catching just a few words of a stranger's discussion. In those cases, it might be a spirit directing your attention to words you need to hear.

- Songs can also be important signals from those we've loved and lost. If you find yourself reminiscing about an old friend, the next song you hear could be one you listened to back when you were together. Is that sort of thing merely a coincidence? I don't think so.

CALLING CARDS

One of my favorite tools for spirit contact is a tarot deck. Tarot cards have a long, rich history. They started as a game, which means they're still a playful method for spirit communication. As centuries passed, the cards were also imbued with layers of meaning and symbolism, ranging from astrology to zodiac symbols.

To get the most from a tarot deck, you'll want to study the cards. Start with the symbols you recognize and expand your research into the myths, legends, and astrological principles associated with the cards.

That doesn't mean you need to be an expert before you can begin. If you're new to tarot but you'd still like to try your hand at spirit readings, begin with the major arcana—the first twenty-two cards of the deck.

When I invite spirits to join me at my tarot table, I shuffle the cards and ask them to show me who they were in life and how they are in the Spirit World. You can also ask them for signs of their continued presence in your life. Simply ask any spirits who are present to reveal themselves through the imagery of the cards, one at a time.

Here are the types of questions I usually ask:

- How would you describe yourself?
- What did you look like?
- How do you feel about your life?
- How did you die?
- What is your focus now?
- Do you have a message you'd like to share?

As you work with the cards for spirit contact, you're sure to come up with similar questions of your own.

CARD MEANINGS

Here's a brief guide to the significance each card might have in a spirit reading. Remember that each card can apply to men, women, and children alike.

- The Fool: A soul in search of experience, a happy wanderer, a naive beginner, an adventurer. *Astrological association: the rebel planet Uranus, primordial god of the sky, ruler of Aquarius.*

- The Magician: A quick thinker, fast talker, salesman, trickster, possibly a thief. *Astrological association: Mercury, the messenger of the gods, the closest companion to the sun, ruler of Gemini.*

- The High Priestess: A trusted confidant, wise counselor, soft-spoken advisor. *Astrological association: the luminous Moon, goddess of the night, reflective ruler of Cancer.*

- The Empress: A mother, artist, creator, and unstoppable force of nature. A lover, not a fighter. *Astrological association: the shining planet Venus, goddess of love, ruler of earthy Taurus and airy Libra.*

- The Emperor: A bold leader, accomplished ruler, successful entrepreneur, honored military man. *Astrological association: Aries, the ram, the fiery sign of leadership and drive, ruled by Mars.*

- The Hierophant: A teacher, professor, minister, or priest. *Astrological association: Taurus, the bull, the earthy sign of strength and stability, ruled by Venus.*

- The Lovers: Kindred spirits, soulmates, siblings, lifelong friends, and companions. Talkative, curious, easily distracted. *Astrological association: Gemini, the twins, the airy sign of communication and curiosity, ruled by Mercury.*

- The Chariot: A warrior, patriot, soldier, defender, police officer, or protective mother. *Astrological association: Cancer, the crab, the watery sign of home and family, ruled by the Moon.*

- Strength: A brave fighter, a courageous first responder, a winning athlete, sports enthusiast, and flirt. *Astrological association: Leo, the lion, the fiery sign of recreation and play, ruled by the Sun.*

- The Hermit: A loner, old soul, solitary figure, and wise mentor. Meticulous, conscientious, precise, and regimented. A stickler for detail. A proofreader, editor, or librarian. *Astrological association: Virgo, the virgin, the earthy sign of duty and responsibility, ruled by Mercury.*

- The Wheel of Fortune: An optimist, risk-taker, and freethinker. A world traveler. A philosopher, publisher, professor. A benefactor. *Astrological association: the expansive planet Jupiter, the great benefic, king of the gods, ruler of Sagittarius.*

- Justice: An idealist. A negotiator, lawyer, or judge. Likes to socialize and organize parties and special events. *Astrological association: Libra, the scales, the airy sign of grace and balance, ruled by Venus.*

- The Hanged Man: Selfless, meditative, contemplative. Possibly spent time in an altered state. *Astrological association: the misty planet Neptune, god of the sea, ruler of watery Pisces.*

- Death: Fascinated by mystery and cosmic secrets. An undertaker, gravedigger, psychologist, psychiatrist. *Astrological association: Scorpio, the scorpion, the watery sign of mysteries and secrets, ruled by Pluto.*

- Temperance: A spirit guide, guardian angel. A mixologist. A scientist. *Astrological association: Sagittarius, the archer, the fiery sign of adventure and exploration, ruled by Jupiter.*

- The Devil: An earthbound angel. A successful businessman, banker, investor. May have battled drug or alcohol addiction. *Astrological association: Capricorn, the goat, the earthy sign of business, career, and social status, ruled by Saturn.*

- The Tower: A rebel, activist, mover and shaker. A firefighter, first responder, or member of an invading army. A prisoner or prison guard. A victim of a natural disaster. *Astrological association: The red planet Mars, god of war, ruler of Aries.*

- The Star: An optimist, idealist, utopian visionary. A reformer, inventor, or technological genius. *Astrological association: Aquarius, the Water Bearer, the airy sign of visionary thinking, ruled by Uranus.*

- The Moon: A dreamer, mystic, and deeply reflective soul. One who craves escape from everyday reality. A caregiver or patient, a convict or guard. *Astrological association: Pisces, the fish, the watery sign of depth and connection, ruled by Neptune.*

- The Sun: The star of any show. A celebrity, actor, musician, performer, spokesperson, photographer. *Astrological association: the golden sun, the god Apollo, ruler of Leo.*

- Judgement: A literal judge, teacher, minister, authority figure, or musician. *Astrological association: Pluto, god of the underworld, ruler of Scorpio.*

- The World: A world traveler, dancer, carpenter, or builder. *Astrological association: the ringed planet Saturn, god of time, ruler of Capricorn.*

IS YOUR HOUSE HAUNTED?

Is your house haunted? Here are the top ten signs, all of which we've experienced firsthand at the Haunted Antique Shop.

1. Doors open and close on their own. At the shop, we check the latches to make sure doors are firmly shut. It doesn't matter, though, because they seem to open by themselves when we're not looking.

2. In the same way, lights turn on and off. We check the bulbs, the fuses, and the plugs; nothing can explain it.

3. Voices echo in empty rooms. Sometimes, you might simply hear a whisper. At other times, there could be an audible greeting—like the "hey" we hear from James in the kitchenette. You

might even hear spirit voices that seem to be engaged in conversation with each other.

4. Footsteps ricochet across floorboards when no one else is in the building. You could also hear other noises you can't explain, like thumps, bumps, and mysterious creaking.

5. Inanimate objects move on their own, like Lucinda's rocking chair that slowly sways back and forth, or Haunted Charlie, who can't keep his hands still.

6. Fleeting shadows and reflections appear and disappear, separate from any obvious light source.

7. Phantom aromas come and go. Some of the most common scents include perfume and tobacco.

8. Items mysteriously disappear then reappear in unexpected places. Once, I misplaced my wedding ring and tore the house apart looking for it. A few days later, my daughter found it in a purse I hadn't used for months. "I prayed to Grandma Hansen," she said, "and she showed me where it was."

9. Because spirits need physical energy to move and manifest, they sometimes leave cold spots in their wake. Paranormal researchers use meters to detect dramatic temperature changes when they investigate haunted houses.

10. Animals react to visitors only they can see and hear. We don't have pets at the Haunted Antique Shop, but our landlord's wife, Linda, once did. "Our cats were never happy here," she told me. "They could never settle down. When they weren't hissing at something in the corner, they just ran from one room to another."

As you look for signs of hauntings, remember that most odd experiences have perfectly logical explanations. Not every bump in the night is a ghost. At the Haunted Antique Shop, for example, our floors are old, and some of the boards creak when you step on them. They're not perfectly level, either, which means some display shelves shake a little when you walk past. And just like anywhere, you might smell cigarette smoke from the guys across the street, see lights glint from passing cars, or hear creepy little footsteps from squirrels on the roof. It all adds to the haunted appeal of the place, but we'll be the first to tell you when your experience is normal, not paranormal.

Image 93: "Memories of the Past," a stereographic photo from 1880.

We'll even tell you the truth when you stand in front of the Cabinet of Curiosities and you suddenly sense a rush of cold air swirling through the room. If you're mesmerized by the merchandise and you get chills, that might just be the air conditioning underneath the armoire.

CLEANING HOUSE

Years ago, I lived in a three-bedroom rambler, a mid-century modern house from 1954. It didn't look like a haunted house. It wasn't a creepy old Victorian with turrets and towers and a widow's walk wrapping around a third-story attic. It was just a boxy rectangle, with a front door in the center and windows on either side, almost like a child's drawing of a house. It was cute and it was functional, but it wasn't the sort of place you'd drive by and think, "Wow, I bet that house has some stories to tell."

Image 94: A Florida firefighter poses with a broom used to thrash burning embers, circa 1890.

And yet, it sat vacant for months before we bought it, when other houses were selling as soon as they hit the market.

About a year after I moved in, my neighbor Barbara came over for coffee and raved about how good the house felt. I know I must have looked at her funny. "What do you mean?" I asked.

"Before you moved in," she said, "there was just something really creepy about this house. I walked through when it was up for sale, and I couldn't wait to get out. I felt like someone was watching us the whole time. It seemed like there should be an old woman in the living room, creaking back and forth in a rocking chair like Norman Bates's mother in *Psycho* or something."

I kind of wished I could have seen that—but a part of me was glad I hadn't. It sounded so different from the house I had come to know and love. All I could do was shrug.

As far as I know, no one had ever died in that house—but houses don't have to be the scene of tragedy to be haunted. Even a death in a house doesn't necessarily condemn the soul who died there to linger forever. But any form of distress could leave traces. Have you ever walked into a room where two people have been arguing? Even if they stop the minute they see you, the air is usually thick with tension. That sort of energy can linger, whether it originates in anger, sadness, grief, loss, or disappointment.

If your home or workspace feels as though it's shrouded in negativity, you can clean it out and replace it with lighter, brighter energy. Here's what I recommend:

- Starting at the front of your house, open all your doors and windows. Leave them open as long as possible so fresh air can blow through.

- As your house airs out, dust, sweep, and vacuum. Play music and sing while you work to fill the space with joyful sound and emotions. If you don't have time to clean your whole house, just take out the trash from every room, along with some of the clutter. This is a symbolic process, so do what you can.

- Imagine that the dirt and debris you collect actually holds most of the negativity you'd like to remove. Don't leave it sitting in a trash can where you'll have to live with it, even overnight. Take it out through the back door and imagine all that negativity leaving your home for good.

- Starting at your front door, refill your space with positive energy. Burn incense or bundles of sage, or spritz holy water or essential oil in every room. As you bless every area, pray or recite an affirmation like "May this be a place of peace" or "May all who enter here find health and happiness within."

- Open all the doors in every room, including closets and cabinets, and bless the space inside. Don't overlook dark, shadowy spaces you don't normally visit, like basements, attics, and garages.
- Picture your home, your loved ones, and your belongings bathed in a protective sphere of bright, white light. Imagine that light as a force field, impermeable to anyone who would break in or harm you.
- If you suspect that an unhappy ghost is in one of the areas you're trying to clear, ask your own guardian angels and spirit guides to step in. Invite them to intercede, to comfort any lost souls and help them to a better place. They'll do the heavy lifting; all you have to do is ask.
- When you're done, light a candle and bask in the energy of a clean, comfortable home.

MEMORY LANE

Have you ever found yourself walking down a quiet street in a historic neighborhood and realized that you could be standing in the same place at any time in history? Maybe it's because you're surrounded by old buildings, essentially unchanged for decades. Maybe it's because the sunlight is filtering through the trees, just as you remember from your childhood. Maybe it's simply déjà vu ... or maybe you are truly tapping into another time.

If you recognize that sensation, it's one you can use to reconnect with loved ones too. Here's a guided meditation that truly does work wonders.

Close your eyes and picture yourself on a peaceful, tree-lined street. You might be in a quiet small town like DeLand, a charming boulevard in Paris, or a walking path in New York's Central Park. Wherever you find yourself, you feel safe and relaxed.

Look around, and you'll see a comfortable place to sit. It could be a park bench, a picnic blanket on the lawn, or a table at a sidewalk café.

Have a seat and enjoy the warmth of the sun on your skin. Breathe deeply and notice the scent of flowers in the air. Relax your body and your mind.

Image 95: DeLand's main street has always been picturesque.

As you keep breathing slowly, you might feel a ripple in the space-time continuum. A sudden burst of sunlight could break through the clouds. A misty patch of fog might rise up from the ground in front of you. You might feel a warm breeze brushing across your skin.

In that moment, the person you most want to see will be standing in front of you. That person might embrace you, take your hand, or simply sit down next to you with a smile.

Keep your eyes closed and enjoy how good it feels to spend time together.

This is a meditation, which means you can communicate telepathically. Say anything you like and be open to receiving a message from your loved one too.

You can even give and receive symbolic gifts. What would you offer as a token of your affection? What would your person give you in return? You might be surprised at the exchange.

Most importantly, what do you wish you could say to that person?

You can reach out any time. When you meet in spirit, it's never too late to be together.

HEAVEN CAN WAIT: WHY DO WE LIKE GHOSTS?

You might think that with all our focus on ghosts, we're obsessed with death. In fact, the opposite is true. Ghosts remind us of the joys of being alive. Some of those pleasures are purely physical. While we're in our bodies, we can eat, drink, and be merry.

First Plane to land in DeLand Fla
C.T. Kruse

Image 96: Adventurers began to fly in and out of DeLand during the 1920s.

Other gratifications are grounded in our relationships. Ghosts remind us to make the most of our time with friends and family members now, while we can. After we're gone, it won't be as easy to reach out and touch the ones we love.

Ghosts also remind us that we are eternal. Our sole purpose—and our soul's purpose—isn't merely to walk the earth. We're here to make a difference, to touch the lives of others, and build relationships that transcend time and space.

Along the way, ghosts help us find our place in history. When we reach out to shadows of the past, we establish a direct connection with those

who came before—as well as those who will follow in our footsteps someday in the future, when we ourselves are distant memories.

Ghosts offer reassurance that our lives have meaning and that we're not
fleeting sparks that will burn brightly and then fall back to earth as ashes or
as dust. Ghosts remind us that a life well lived will never end but continue
to hold value for as long as some trace of our existence remains to mark
our place.

Someday, we know we'll all be freed from the bonds of time and space.
We'll be liberated from the bonds of our earthly forms and released from
our gravitational ties to this planet. For now, however, heaven can wait;
we're perfectly happy to remain souls in physical form.

CONCLUSION

I had the craziest dream as I was putting the finishing touches on this manuscript. One morning, just before I woke up, I dreamed I saw all the ghosts of DeLand having a street dance downtown.

Everyone was there: Henry DeLand, John Stetson, our resident spirits, and all the other ghosts you've met in this book. There were even a few who didn't make the final cut—like Miss Hettie, who started the first church in DeLand; Rowena Dean, the first teacher; and Ruben Marsh, the first settler to stake a claim in the general area. I couldn't fit everyone in, but maybe some of them will show up on my blog or in my shop.

As the old pioneers danced, they laughed and smiled and high-fived each other, bouncing and stomping along in a choreographed series of steps as if they were in a big-screen musical. They clapped their hands and celebrated, dancing for joy at the fact that they would be immortalized in this book.

I woke up laughing too. It feels good to make old ghosts happy.

I've enjoyed telling you about the Haunted Antique Shop, but it's time to close the final chapter—at least for now.

In the coming months and years, we'll keep adding to our collection of stories and reports. Some will probably show up on our website. If you come to the shop, maybe one of your experiences will even make it into a revised and expanded edition of this text.

Image 97: Atlantic Coast Line Railroad employees with steam engine 643 in DeLand, circa 1910.

In the meantime, every day is another opportunity to make contact with the Spirit World—and to share stories of your interactions with ghosts.

Let's stay in touch. You can find me on the web and on social media; just look for the Haunted Antique Shop. Friend us, follow us, and tag us. And if you happen to be in Central Florida, please stop in and see us!

PHOTO CREDITS

All photos courtesy of the author except from:

Athens Theater: 37

Bill Alkofer, courtesy of Katherine Kenner: 77

Courtney and Kelly Conova: 63

Dutton House Inc.: 64

Katherine Kenner: 18, 79

Library of Congress: 60, 69, 81, 84, 93

State Archives of Florida: 16, 32, 33b, 33c, 34, 35, 38–41, 55, 88, 89, 92, 94, 96, 97

Stetson University Library: 30, 31, 42, 44, 45, 47, 51, 57, 67

Wayne Kenner: 70

West Volusia Historical Society: 5, 24, 26–28, 33a, 49, 50, 52, 53, 56, 62, 65, 80

William LaMartin: 68

BIBLIOGRAPHY

DELAND HISTORY

Caccamise, Louise Ball. *Memory Lane: A History of the Street Names of DeLand, Florida.* DeLand, FL: West Volusia Historical Society, 2013.

DeLand—The Next 30 Years: 1890–1920. Narrated by Bill Dreggors. Produced by Charles Van Alen. Video recording. DeLand, FL: West Volusia Historical Society, 1999.

DeLand City Directories, R. L. Polk & Co., Jacksonville, Florida, 1924–1936.

DeLand, Helen Parce. *Story of DeLand and Lake Helen Florida.* Norwich, CT: The Academy Press, 1928.

DeLand Revisited. Narrated by Bill Dreggors. Video recording. DeLand, FL: West Volusia Historical Society, 1999.

The Founding of a City: Henry A. DeLand, 1876. Narrated by Bill Dreggors. Produced by Charles Van Alen. Video recording. DeLand, FL: West Volusia Historical Society, 1999.

Francke, Arthur E., Jr., Alyce Hockaday Gillingham, and Maxine Carey Turner. *Volusia: The West Side.* DeLand, FL: West Volusia Historical Society, 1986.

French, Larry. *Florida Stories: Walk DeLand*. St. Petersburg, FL: Florida Humanities Council, 2016.

Hall, Maggi Smith, Michael Justin Holder, and the West Volusia Historical Society. *DeLand*. Images of America. Charleston, SC: Arcadia Publishing, 2003.

Haught, Karen and Wayne Carter. *DeLand Historic Mural Walk*. DeLand, FL: MainStreet DeLand Association, 2016.

Johnston, Sidney. "Historical Structure Form, Record Number 217, Site 8-VO-3681." Florida Master Site File. St. Augustine, Florida: Historic Property Associates, Inc., 1991.

Roberts, L. Thomas, and the West Volusia Historical Society. *DeLand*. Postcard History Series. Charleston, SC: Arcadia Publishing, 2014.

Ryder, Karen. *Better Country Beyond: The Amazing Cinderella Story of the Early Pioneers of DeLand, Florida*. DeLand, FL: West Volusia Historical Society, 2019.

Schene, Michael G. *Hopes, Dreams, and Promises: A History of Volusia County, Florida*. Daytona Beach, FL: News-Journal Corporation, 1976.

Shiver, W. Carl. "Downtown DeLand Historic District." United States Department of the Interior, National Park Service, National Register of Historic Places Inventory—Nomination Form. Florida Bureau of Historic Preservation, Tallahassee, Florida, 1987.

Smith, Dusty. *Haunted DeLand and the Ghosts of West Volusia County*. Charleston, SC: Haunted America, 2008.

A Souvenir of the City of DeLand, Florida. DeLand, Florida: News Publishing Company, 1902. Accessed via the University of Florida Digital Collections, George A. Smathers Libraries, Gainesville, Florida. https://ufdc.ufl.edu/UF00004127/00001.

Volusia County Eco Tourism. "DeLand Historical Trail." Accessed July 2021. http://maps1.vcgov.org/EcoTourism/HistoricWalkTour/DELAND.pdf.

Williamson, Ronald W. *Volusia County's West Side: Steamboats & Sandhills*. Charleston, SC: The History Press, 2008.

THE HAUNTED HISTORY OF DELAND

Balzano, Christopher. *Haunted Florida Love Stories*. Charleston, SC: Arcadia Publishing, 2020.

"Paranormal America 2018: Chapman University Survey of American Fears." Chapman University. October 16, 2018. https://blogs.chapman.edu/wilkinson/2018/10/16/paranormal-america-2018/.

Peace, Suze. "Ghost Walks of Historic DeLand." Ghost tour script. West Volusia Historical Society, DeLand, Florida, 1995.

Smith, Dusty. *Haunted DeLand and the Ghosts of West Volusia County*. Charleston, SC: Haunted America, 2008.

PERMANENT RESIDENTS: THE RICH FAMILY

McKee, James Harvey. *Back "In War Times.": History of the 144th Regiment, New York Volunteer Infantry [...]*. Unadilla, NY: H. E. Bailey, 1903.

New York State Division of Military and Naval Affairs. "144th Infantry Civil War Roster." Latham, New York. https://dmna.ny.gov/historic/reghist/civil/rosters/Infantry/144th_Infantry_CW_Roster.pdf.

OUR FOUNDING FATHER, HENRY DELAND

"The Great Freeze of 1894–1895." Orange County Regional History Center. Historical Society of Central Florida. December 28, 2017. https://www.thehistorycenter.org/the-big-chill/.

Johnston, Sidney. "Two for Stetson: How Two Philanthropists Helped the Early University." *Stetson University Magazine* 31, no 3. (Winter 2015): 40–41. https://issuu.com/stetsonu/docs/stetson-magazine-31-3/43.

McMurry, Charles Alexander. *Type Studies from the Geography of the United States: First Series*. United Kingdom, Macmillan, 1904.

Schroeder, Jessa. "Little Known Details Surrounding the 1876 Brooklyn Theatre Fire that Killed Hundreds of People." *New York Daily News*. December 5, 2016. https://www.nydailynews.com/new-york/brooklyn/details-surrounding-1876-brooklyn-theater-fire-article-1.2894524.

"Was Founder of Town in Florida: Henry Addison DeLand, of Fairport, Dies." *Rochester Democrat and Chronicle*. March 14, 1908. https://www .newspapers.com/image/?clipping_id=4180474&fcfToken=eyJhbGciOi JIUzI1NiIsInR5cCI6IkpXVCJ9.eyJmcmVlLXZpZXctaWQiOjEzNTQ2M jczOSwiaWF0IjoxNjQ2ODU1OTE0LCJleHAiOjE2NDY5NDIzMTR9 .Jvc-PxbJ5mQ1nL0LyZIq9WigcYJtoQNb5WxV0hgA9qc.

THE PHILANTHROPIST, JOHN B. STETSON

Bowen, Olga. *History of Stetson University*. Oral history, transcribed 1967. Stetson University Library Archives, DeLand, FL. https://www2 .stetson.edu/library/green/wp-content/uploads/2014/01/alumni _bowen.pdf.

Gordis, Warren Stone. *John B. Stetson University: History and Reminiscences*. Manuscript, 1948. Stetson University Library Archives, DeLand, FL.

Longstreet, Rupert James. "Stetson Decade: 1907–1917. An Account of Stetson University as I Saw It." Manuscript, 1950. Stetson University Library, file AZ43.L66 S74.

Lycan, Gilbert L. *Stetson University: The First 100 Years*. DeLand, FL: Stetson University Press, 1983.

Ryan, Susan M. "John B. Stetson: A Hatter Legacy." Stetson University Library Archives, DeLand, Florida, 2016.

Ryan, Susan M. "No Rubbish: A 125th Anniversary History of Stetson University's Libraries." Stetson University Library Archives, DeLand, Florida, 2008.

GHOSTS OF THE GILDED AGE

Solari, Michael. *Where Did You Come From? The Inspiring Inside Story about a House That Changes Lives*. Self-published, DeLand, FL, 2014.

Thompson, J. T. *How to Polish a Diamond*. Self-published, DeLand, FL, 2014.

OUT OF THE ASHES: DELAND'S GREAT FIRE

"Crawford Peter Wilcox." Find a Grave. Accessed March 9, 2022. https://www.findagrave.com/memorial/41320785/crawford-peter -wilcox.

DeLand, Helen Parce. *Story of DeLand and Lake Helen Florida*. Norwich, CT: The Academy Press, 1928.

ENCORE PERFORMANCES AT THE ATHENS THEATRE

Baldwin, Alexa. Athens Theatre Executive Director, DeLand, Florida. Interview by Corrine Kenner, July 13, 2021.

"History." Athens Theatre. Accessed April 18, 2022. https://athensdeland .com/about/history/.

THE HOTEL PUTNAM

Bulit, David. "Putman Hotel." Abandoned Florida. Accessed July 2021. https://www.abandonedfl.com/putnam-hotel/.

Carpenter, John W. "Putnam Hotel DeLand." *The Unforgotten Man: William James Carpenter* (blog). WordPress. Accessed July 2021. https://jackncb .wordpress.com/architecture/deland-area/putnam-hotel-deland.

SCHOOL SPIRITS AT STETSON UNIVERSITY

"Beckerath Organ Turns 50." Stetson Today. October 21, 2011. https:// www2.stetson.edu/today/2011/10/50th-anniversary-of-stetson -beckerath-organ-nov-4-5/.

Hall, Maggi Smith. *Stetson University*. The Campus History Series. Charleston, SC: Arcadia Publishing, 2005.

Hertz, Noah. "Haunted History Tour Walks Stetson Students through Campus Frights." *The West Volusia Beacon*. October 31, 2020. https:// beacononlinenews.com/2020/10/31/haunted-history-tour-walks -stetson-students-through-campus-frights/.

Hulley, Lincoln. *Fables and Myths from the Sibyl's Book*. DeLand, FL: Press of the E. O. Painter Printing Company, 1925.

Jalowitz, Alan. "Lincoln Hulley." Literary & Cultural Maps of PA. Pennsylvania Center for the Book. The Pennsylvania State University. 2006. https://pabook.libraries.psu.edu/literary-cultural-heritage-map-pa /bios/Hulley__Lincoln.

Larson, Kelly. Archivist, Archives & Special Collections, duPont-Ball Library, Stetson University, DeLand, Florida. Interview by Corrine Kenner, July 12, 2021.

Murphy, Hunter. Engagement and Learning Librarian, duPont-Ball Library, Stetson University, DeLand, Florida. Interview by Corrine Kenner, July 12, 2021.

Shiver, W. Carl. "Stetson University Campus Historic District." United States Department of the Interior, National Park Service, National Register of Historic Places Registration Form. Bureau of Historic Preservation, Tallahassee, Florida, 1990.

Vandiver, Margaret. "The Quality of Mercy: Race and Clemency in Florida Death Penalty Cases." *University of Richmond Law Review* 27, no. 2 (1993): 1924–1966. https://scholarship.richmond.edu/lawreview /vol27/iss2/9/.

LIVING HISTORY: THE FARRISS FAMILY AT THE DELAND HOUSE MUSEUM

Allen, William Sims, et al. "In Loving Memory of Charles Sherwood Farriss: School Mourns Demise of Dr. Farriss." *The Stetson Reporter*, April 27, 1938.

Alma Farriss Obituary. "Mrs. Farriss Dies in Durham, N.C." *DeLand Sun News*, August 30, 1944.

Charles Farriss Obituary. "Dr. Charles Farriss, Florida Educator." *The New York Times*, April 15, 1938.

Lycan, Gilbert L. *Charles Sherwood Farriss: 1856–1938*. Manuscript in the archives of the West Volusia Historical Society, dated January 15, 1986.

Thorncroft, Sarah. Executive Director, West Volusia Historical Society, DeLand, Florida. Interview by Corrine Kenner, July 10, 2021.

THE WIZARD'S DEATH MASK

Aronson, Virginia. *Gift of the Unicorn: The Story of Lue Gim Gong, Florida's Citrus Wizard.* Sarasota, FL: Pineapple Press, 2002.

Daytona Beach News-Journal Editorial. "Chinese Citrus Grower Deserves DeLand Honor." *Daytona Beach News-Journal.* July 21, 1998. https://www.news-journalonline.com/story/opinion/editorials/2021/05/22/lue-gim-gong-delands-citrus-wizard-asked-little-and-gave-much-florida-orange/5210077001/.

Dickinson, Joy Wallace. "'Citrus Wizard' Merits Place in Hall of Fame." *Orlando Sentinel.* September 30, 2018. https://www.orlandosentinel.com/features/os-joy-wallace-dickinson-0930-story.html.

"Lue Gim Gong, DeLand's 'Citrus Wizard,' Saved an Industry and Asked Little in Return." *The Daytona Beach News-Journal.* May 22, 2021. https://www.news-journalonline.com/story/opinion/editorials/2021/05/22/lue-gim-gong-delands-citrus-wizard-asked-little-and-gave-much-florida-orange/5210077001/.

"Lue Gim Gong Honored by Savants; Gentle Chinese in Florida Won Medal for New Orange—A Master in His Field." *The New York Times.* June 21, 1925. https://www.nytimes.com/1925/06/21/archives/lue-gim-gong-honored-by-savants-gentle-chinese-in-florida-won-medal.html.

Poertner, Bo. "Plant Wizard and His Oranges Are Gone, but Memories of Him Bloom." *Orlando Sentinel.* April 16, 1998. https://www.orlandosentinel.com/news/os-xpm-1998-04-16-9804160068-story.html.

Williamson, Ronald. "DeLand Pays Tribute to the Man behind a Mask." *The Daytona Beach News-Journal.* September 25, 1999. https://www.news-journalonline.com/story/opinion/editorials/2021/05/22/lue-gim-gong-delands-citrus-wizard-asked-little-and-gave-much-florida-orange/5210077001/.

Zhang, Wenxian. "Lue Gim Gong: A Chinese American Pioneer and the Citrus Wizard of Florida." Rollins Archives. Rollins College. May 5,

2021. https://blogs.rollins.edu/libraryarchives/2021/05/12/lue-gim
-gong-a-chinese-american-pioneer-and-the-citrus-wizard-of-florida/.

JUSTICE IS SERVED: VOLUSIA COUNTY'S HISTORIC COURTHOUSE

Bohon, Sally Landis. "Sands of Time: Hearing Voices on Indiana Avenue."
The West Volusia Beacon. July 1, 2019. https://beacononlinenews.com
/2019/07/01/sands-of-time-hearing-voices-on-indiana-avenue/.

Franklin, Benjamin. "The Morals of Chess." *The Papers of Benjamin Franklin*. Vol. 29: March 1 through June 30, 1779. Edited by Barbara B. Oberg.
New Haven, CT: Yale University Press, 1992.

Johnston, Sidney. "Bert Fish: From Volusia County Courthouse to American Embassy." *The Florida Historical Quarterly* 78, no. 4 (Spring 2000):
430–50. https://www.jstor.org/stable/30149181.

"One Law Firm … A History of Experience." Landis, Graham, French,
P.A., Attorneys at Law. Accessed July 1, 2021. https://www.landispa
.com/about-us/our-history.

Youngblood, E. Garrett. "Ropes was DeLand's Eccentric." *Orlando Sentinel*.
January 17, 2001. https://www.orlandosentinel.com/news/os-xpm
-2001-01-17-0101170453-story.html.

THE HANGED MAN: CHECKMATE AT CHESS PARK

Bishop, Bernard. "At DeLand Jail: State's Final Execution By Hanging
Began With Sheriff's Brief Query, 'Charlie Brown, Are You Ready?'"
DeLand Sun News, March 8, 1964.

Bres, Rose Falls. "The Charge, Sentence and Execution of Charles Browne
Perelli." *Women Lawyers Journal* 15, no. 2 (April 1927), https://
heinonline.org/HOL/LandingPage?handle=hein.journals/wolj15&div
=16&id=&page=.

Lane, Mark. "90 Years Ago in DeLand, Crowds Watched Florida's Last
Hanging." *The Daytona Beach News-Journal*. April 20, 2017.

YOUR HOSTS, THE BARNHILL GHOSTS

French, Larry. *Grand Hotels of West Volusia County*. Images of America. Charleston, SC: Arcadia Publishing, 2018.

Koslow, Bob. "DeLand Hotel Adds Nightclub, Sports Bar." *The Daytona Beach News-Journal*. December 24, 2011. https://www.news-journal online.com/story/news/2011/12/25/deland-hotel-adds-nightclub -sports-bar/30567841007/.

Smith, Dusty. *Haunted DeLand and the Ghosts of West Volusia County*. Charleston, SC: Arcadia Publishing, 2008.

THE HAUNTED MANSION

Bulit, David. "John Dutton House." Abandoned Florida. Accessed March 9, 2022. https://www.abandonedfl.com/john-dutton-house/.

Copelon, Dianne. "History Buff Saves DeLand's Dutton House." *Orlando Sentinel*. September 11, 1993. https://www.orlandosentinel.com/news /os-xpm-1993-09-11-9309111039-story.html.

Robertson, Dagny. Spokesperson, Dutton House, Inc., DeLand, Florida. Interview by Corrine Kenner, August 23, 2021.

NIGHT SHIFT: DELAND'S MEMORIAL HOSPITAL MUSEUM

McCarthy, Kevin M. *African American Sites in Florida*. Sarasota, FL: Pineapple Press, 2019.

Peace, Suze. West Volusia Historical Society. Interview by Corrine Kenner, July 16, 2021.

West Volusia Historical Society. "White Coats and Caring Hearts." DeLand, Florida, 2019. https://www.delandhouse.com/cemetery _walk_characters.

CASSADAGA, THE PSYCHIC CAPITAL OF THE WORLD

Guthrie Jr., John J., Phillip Charles Lucas, and Gary Monroe, eds. *Cassadaga: The South's Oldest Spiritualist Community*. Gainesville, FL: University Press of Florida, 2000.

Jones, Rev. Maeda. "Southern Cassadaga Spiritualist Camp Visitor's Guide." Southern Cassadaga Spiritualist Camp Meeting Association, Cassadaga, Florida, 2020.

GHOSTS AND SPIRITS

Aquinas, Thomas. *The "Summa Theologica" of St. Thomas Aquinas.* Translated by Fathers of the English Dominican Province. London: Burns, Oates & Washbourne, 1921.

Halliwell, Nick. "Groupon Halloween Survey: More Than 60 Percent of People Have Seen a Ghost." October 19, 2018. https://www.businesswire.com/news/home/20181010005634/en.

TO WRITE TO THE AUTHOR

NOTES

NOTES

NOTES